¡Viva el Español!

Annotated Teacher's Edition

Ava Belisle-Chatterjee
Linda West Tibensky
Abraham Martínez-Cruz

National Textbook Company
a division of *NTC Publishing Group* • Lincolnwood, Illinois USA

ACKNOWLEDGMENTS

The authors wish to acknowledge the administration of Oak Park, Illinois, Districts 97 and 200, and Sabin Magnet School District 6, Chicago, Illinois, for their support and encouragement during the development of the *¡Viva el español!* program.

Project Director: *Keith Fry*

Project Managers: *William Hrabrick, Frank Crane Publishing Services International, Inc.*

Contributing Writer: *Judy Veramendi*

Art & Design Director: *Karen Christoffersen*

Design Manager: *Linda Shum*

Design Concept: *Rosa + Wesley Design Associates*

Cover Design: *Rosa + Wesley Design Associates*

Textbook Page Design: *Fulcrum Creative*

Teacher's Edition Page Design: *Cristina Hiraldo*

Art & Production Coordinator: *Nancy Ellis*

Cover Photographer: *Robert Keeling*

Cover Illustrator: *Terri Starrett*

Illustrators: *Lisa Ansted, Franklin Ayers, Tim Basaldua, James Buckley, Mickey Gill, Carolyn Gruber, David Herrick, Nancy Panacionne, Jon Pickard, Leanne Thomas, Don Wilson, Fred Womack*

Published by National Textbook Company, a division of NTC Publishing Group, 4255 West Touhy Avenue, Lincolnwood (Chicago), Illinois 60646-1975 U.S.A.

Consulting Educators for the *¡Viva el español!* Program

Senior Consultant:

Dr. Gladys C. Lipton
Director, National FLES* Institute
University of Maryland, Baltimore County

Test Designers

Stanley W. Connell
Martha Lucía Torres

Test Consultant

Jean D'Arcy Maculaitis

Pilot Testing

Friedrich L. Jahn
Elementary School
Chicago Public Schools
Chicago, Illinois
Supervising Teacher:
Abraham Martínez-Cruz

New Sabin Magnet School,
District 6
Chicago Public Schools
Chicago, Illinois
Supervising Teacher:
Zulma V. Meléndez

Consultants

Diane Azcoitia
Chicago Public Schools
Chicago, Illinois

Carmen Macías
Assistant Principal
Los Angeles Public Schools
Los Angeles, California

Dr. James Maharg
University of Illinois
Chicago, Illinois

Gloria A. Mariscal
Teacher of Spanish
Eastwood High School
El Paso, Texas

Denise Mesa
Spanish Teacher
Sabal Palm Elementary School
Dade County Public Schools
Miami, Florida

María A. Montalvo
*Coordinator of Modern and
Classical Languages*
Albuquerque Public Schools
Albuquerque, New Mexico

Dr. Francisco Perea
Language Consultant
Austin Independent School
District
Austin, Texas

Elsa Statzner
Spanish FLES Teacher
Longfellow Humanities
Magnet Schools
St. Paul Public Schools
St. Paul, Minnesota

Preface

The *Annotated Teacher's Edition* of *¡Adelante!* forms the core of this innovative, lively program of Spanish as a second language. It contains all the information you will need to plan and implement the program during the school year.

The following are some of the features of the *Annotated Teacher's Edition*:

- Introduction to the *¡Viva el español!* Spanish-language development program
- How-to section for incorporating the program components
- Detailed scope and sequence chart
- Unit-by-unit suggestions for presenting, reviewing, extending, and enriching instruction
- Exercise answers, culture notes, and teaching suggestions printed directly on the pupil edition pages
- Ideas for pacing

Whether you are an experienced teacher or new to the foreign language classroom, this complete *Annotated Teacher's Edition* will help guide, refresh, and inspire you to make students truly say and mean *¡Viva el español!*

CONTENTS

Unit Plans (continued)

T-153   Resource Sections

T-181   Scope and Sequence

Index to Charts and Figures

INTRODUCTION

Overview

¡*Viva el español!* is a six-level program for developing Spanish language proficiency in students from the elementary grades through middle school. Consisting of complete teacher–resource kits—***Learning Systems A, B,*** and ***C***—and a comprehensive textbook series—¡*Hola!, ¿Qué tal?,* and ¡*Adelante!*—the ¡*Viva el español!* program not only teaches language skills but also equips students with learning strategies that will aid them as they continue their studies in later years.

The Learning Systems

Designed specifically for young students, ***Learning Systems A, B,*** and ***C*** develop students' communicative proficiency in listening, speaking, reading, and writing in a gradual, logical progression. Students' language learning becomes a positive, nonthreatening process, similar to the way children acquire their first language. To that end, each multimedia learning system provides components that encourage teachers and students to enjoy the Spanish learning experience.

The integration of the learning system components—puppets, full-color flash cards, stimulating cassettes of songs and activities, full-color posters, picture books, Sharing Books, and animated videos—is explained clearly and in detail in the ***Learning Systems A, B,*** and ***C*** *Teacher's Manuals,* which also include suggestions for the full use of the blackline masters in the *Resource and Activity Book.*

The Textbook Series

The ¡*Viva el español!* textbook series—¡*Hola!, ¿Qué tal?,* and ¡*Adelante!*—has been designed both for those students beginning their Spanish studies (students with no prior Spanish language background) and for those students who have previously acquired some knowledge of Spanish either with the ¡*Viva el español!* learning systems or by some other means.

You will find a thorough discussion of how to use the textbooks with various target groups later in this Introduction.

The textbooks—*¡Hola!*, *¿Qué tal?*, and *¡Adelante!*—develop and refine proficiency while they establish and promote basic language-learning principles through an enthusiastic, lively, and positive approach. The components accompanying the textbooks are carefully integrated to provide all the materials necessary for students' active participation in acquiring Spanish. In addition to the student textbook and this *Annotated Teacher's Edition*, the following components make up each level of the textbook series:

- Workbook
- Workbook, Teacher's Edition
- Lesson Cassettes
- Exercise Cassettes
- Song Cassette
- Overhead Transparencies
- Resource and Activity Book
- Culture Resource Book
- Testing Program (blackline master book of tests with audiocassette)

Goals and Key Features of the *¡Viva el español!* Textbook Series

Objectives

The overall objectives of the *¡Viva el español!* textbook series are to develop, reinforce, and refine proficiency in listening, speaking, reading, writing, and culture. Through an essentially inductive approach, students will gain an understanding of how the language is structured and how they can use this knowledge to express their own needs and talk about the world around them. By developing and refining their skills of observation, students also acquire a basic understanding and appreciation of the diversity of cultures in the Spanish-speaking world.

Time Frame

Each textbook in the series—*¡Hola!*, *¿Qué tal?*, and *¡Adelante!*—contains sufficient instructional material for a full academic year of stimulating thirty- to forty-minute class periods. Each regular unit of the textbooks contains sufficient material for fourteen days of interactive, hands-on learning, with time for evaluation. The elements of the textbooks, the time frame of a sample unit, as well as the Testing Program, will be described in detail later in this *Annotated Teacher's Edition*.

Versatility of Instruction

The design of the textbooks enables you to target the lessons to the abilities and needs of your students. Whether your class is made up of students who are just beginning their studies or of students who have previously acquired some proficiency in Spanish—as well as any combination of the two groups—the multilevel approach of the exercises in the program gives you the flexibility to tailor your instruction to the specific needs of your students.

Three-Level Approach

Both in the textbooks and in the workbooks of *¡Hola!*, *¿Qué tal?*, and *¡Adelante!*, exercises are provided at three different levels. The level is indicated in the *Annotated Teacher's Edition* only. With this hierarchical system, you will know instantly the level for which the exercises are intended. The symbols on the following page appear next to exercises on the annotated pages of the student textbook.

○ **Mechanical.** These exercises consist of simple activities that require minimal manipulation of the language. They generally have single correct answers, and are readily accessible to all students.

◑ **Meaningful.** These exercises require some manipulation of the language within a meaningful context, and generally simulate real conversation. Students are allowed some flexibility within a range of answers. They are frequently set up as paired practice.

● **Communicative.** These exercises and activities require students to express their own preferences, feelings, and thoughts to interact with classmates, either in pairs or in small groups.

Naturally, you may use any or all of the exercises regardless of level, according to the speed at which your students progress. Some students may progress quickly to the more difficult exercises, whereas others may need to spend extra time on the easy exercises for reinforcement or review. In short, the three-level approach has been devised to give you the flexibility you need to respond to the learning styles, abilities, and language-learning backgrounds of your students.

Another purpose of this three-level design is to allow students to focus on essential vocabulary and structures while practicing different language skills. Thus, you can control and vary the pace so that students get the practice they need to build a proper foundation in all the essential proficiencies.

By the end of *¡Adelante!*, the third textbook in the series, all students —whether they began their studies with *¡Hola!* or with the Learning Systems—should have mastered the equivalent of one-plus years of high school Spanish. It is anticipated that students who started with *Learning Systems A, B,* and *C* will demonstrate a greater degree of proficiency and fluency in Spanish than students who have not studied with them.

Communication Orientation

In all aspects of the *¡Viva el español!* program, the emphasis is on communication. Throughout the program, lessons and units begin with the students' world and gradually spiral outward to the communities of the world. In concert with students' naturally developing awareness of their surroundings and the world at large, the communicative functions, language structures, and vocabulary of each textbook enable them to express their own meanings as early as possible.

To encourage and develop students' ability to communicate, exercises, regardless of the level of difficulty, are based in meaningful and communicative contexts. In addition, many of the exercises call for communicative interaction among students, either in pairs or in small groups. Examples of brief communicative exchanges are provided as models for students to use in forming their own conversations. Thus, students may read or listen to an interaction as an example of how the vocabulary or grammar is used in real life; they are never required to memorize or parrot a dialogue. Communication in this sense is the application of language to express meaningful questions, responses, preferences, and opinions.

Methodologies

Throughout the *¡Viva el español!* program, communication and inductive learning are stressed. The various methodologies employed take into consideration different learning and teaching styles. Thus, *¡Viva el español!* uses an eclectic approach, bringing together the best aspects of many teaching methodologies while allowing you to use the ones with which you feel most comfortable.

Foremost among the methodologies incorporated in *¡Viva el español!* are the Natural Approach and Total Physical Response, developed by Tracy Terrell and James Asher, respectively.

The Natural Approach and Total Physical Response approximate in the classroom, as much as is realistically possible, the informal environment of first-language acquisition. Asher, Terrell, and other researchers in the field of foreign language teaching have shown that programs based on the processes of first-language acquisition result in greater retention and a greater ability to create new and meaningful messages. Equally important, foreign-language programs that incorporate these methods have generated a more favorable attitude toward foreign-language study among learners. One reason for the improved attitude is that both methods presuppose that foreign language instruction should meet students' communicative needs. That is, foreign-language programs should help students acquire the vocabulary, phrases, structures, and eventually the grammatical skills appropriate to and useful in their everyday environment. When this has been accomplished, foreign-language study, like first-language acquisition, is considered to be meaningful, useful, and pleasurable.

The Natural Approach

Elements of the Natural Approach to second-language instruction have been implemented throughout the *¡Viva el español!* program. As employed in the program, this approach helps foster spontaneous, nonthreatening, and meaningful communication among students. The key to this approach is that second-language instruction in the school should attempt to parallel the manner in which children learn their first language in the home.

In contrast to traditional methods of second-language instruction, first-language acquisition is a low-stress learning process. It includes an extended period of listening, positive reinforcement, meaningful and effective communication, and a nonthreatening environment.

As children learn to speak at home, they first pass through relatively passive stages of learning in which their responses to the language of their caretakers consist first of physical reactions and simple utterances and later of the generation of complete, grammatical sentences.

Traditional second-language instruction in schools has often consisted of a teacher-centered environment in which beginning students are required to produce completely formulated, error-free responses to the teacher's questions. Also in many traditional classrooms, the actual use of the target language is only a small percentage of the total communication, relegated only to dialogues, readings, and exercises. Thus, students are expected to communicate in a second language to which they have actually received very little exposure. This unnatural atmosphere has often resulted in a high-stress environment and considerable student anxiety, both of which hinder language learning.

In the *¡Viva el español!* Learning Systems and textbook series, the numerous activities, lessons, and units all work together to maximize the students' willingness to communicate while providing a language-rich environment. Unlike the traditional anxiety-producing approaches, *¡Viva el español!* eliminates the fear of failure. Students utter completely formulated sentences only when they are ready and are motivated to communicate meaningful messages. You, as the teacher, become the caretaker, model, and "significant other" in the second-language learning process. Translated into practical terms, you, the caretaker, establish a learning environment with the following characteristics:

◆ Extensive use and examples of the target language in the classroom

◆ Continual positive reinforcement

◆ Low-stress correction of student errors through modeling and by example

◆ Meaningful communication through activities, such as learning games; short questions and comments about everyday activities; in-class recognition of birthdays, achievements, and other events important to students; positive comments on and display of students' work, etc.

◆ A nurturing and positive attitude toward students' efforts and toward the language itself and the cultures of which it is a part

◆ A stimulating, flexible agenda in which students are actively participating in the communication process throughout the class period

In short, you create a learning environment in which the language directly relates to the students and their surroundings and reflects their needs, interests, and everyday life.

Total Physical Response

Closely related to the Natural Approach is Total Physical Response (TPR). TPR promotes the use of nonverbal communication in the acquisition of a second language. As with the Natural Approach, this concept is based on the process by which a first language is acquired, one in which children respond to their caretakers with appropriate physical actions.

As its name implies, TPR in the classroom involves a physical response to a command or direction to help students learn vocabulary and other concepts. Equally important, the physical response and activities help students retain over time what they have learned.

Generally, TPR is used most often in the first stages of learning new words and language concepts, when the emphasis is on the development of listening comprehension and speaking skills. Following this method, students pass through a silent period during which they listen as you say the various TPR commands and then demonstrate the appropriate responses to those commands.

Eventually, students indicate comprehension, not necessarily through speech, but by performing or carrying out the direction or command. Activities associated with TPR are ideal for children and adolescents because they take into consideration the short attention spans and need for physical activity that are characteristic of these age groups.

Typical TPR activities are set up in a four-step process. In the first step, the teacher gives the command and models it several times as students passively observe. Then, in the second step, students respond to the command as a group with the teacher still modeling the appropriate response. As the students' self-confidence increases and after they successfully carry out the commands as a group, the teacher begins the third step by giving commands to individuals. During this step, continued input through modeling is crucial in maintaining a low anxiety level among students. Finally, as students become more familiar with the commands, they are ready for the fourth step in which they give the commands to one another and even create their own variations.

In the Unit Plans section and in the on-page annotations of this *Annotated Teacher's Edition*, you will find specific suggestions for integrating Total Physical Response into instruction.

Language Experience Approach

The Language Experience Approach (LEA), which is part of the Natural Approach, parallels first-language acquisition in that it allows students to absorb the language effortlessly. LEA activities begin with the students' active participation in a student-centered, communicative, low-stress activity. Thus, LEA activities carry through and expand on the key elements of the *¡Viva el español!* program—namely, meaningful and comprehensible communication in a positive, language-rich environment.

Through LEA, students develop reading and writing skills by using language that relates to their own experiences. Normally, you begin LEA activities relating to a lesson when students are in the final stages of internalizing the vocabulary and structures. At the final stage, students are comfortable with the new words and structures and are ready to use them freely in the course of a language experience.

A typical LEA activity may begin with a simple role-play activity, a skit, an interactive exercise, or even an in-class project or a class field trip. The activity continues under your guidance with a discussion of the language experience. Initially, this guidance may take the form of asking questions; the discussion takes the form of verbal responses. As students acquire more language, and more confidence in using the language, your role becomes one of facilitator or moderator of a discussion group.

As the discussion of the experience continues, you write key sentences on the chalkboard or on a transparency for students to read. From the outset, students are reading passages that are meaningful and comprehensible to them because they created the passages.

Once a passage, or coherent series of sentences, has been developed, students practice their reading skills first through choral readings and then through individual readings. Willingness to read aloud is enhanced when students know that others are reading with them and when they feel secure in the knowledge that their efforts, though not perfect, will be met with a positive, nurturing response from the teacher.

From reading aloud, students then progress to reading a neat handwritten or typewritten copy of the passage. This copy of the passage can be used for a number of activities. For example, it may be cut into sentence strips for students to put the individual parts or sentences back into a whole passage. The passage may also be used to create a "Big Book" in which students illustrate and assemble the sentences in a book form.

Big Book Activities

Big Book activities promote a positive sense of achievement in students. The Big Books themselves become concrete examples of the students' communication in the language which they can share with their peers and even take home to share with their families. Big Books also provide continual reinforcement. For example, they may be displayed and used for an in-class lending library or even as a special display in the school library. A Big Book review page may be attached to the back for fellow students to write their comments or reviews. Many of the interactive exercises, as well as the situational story exercises, found in the textbook series can form the basis of LEA Big Books. Throughout *¡Hola!*, *¿Qué tal?*, and *¡Adelante!* you will find suggestions for incorporating Big Book activities in the lessons. Students may convert an interactive classroom activity into a story or they may create graphs and charts from the numerous "in-class surveys" that appear in the exercise sections. Students may also build a story around one of the colorful photographs in the textbooks. In short, ample opportunities for LEA activities are provided in the textbooks to stimulate meaningful communication.

| **Functional-Notional Approaches** | Built into the *¡Viva el español!* program are opportunities for students to begin learning and practicing simple functions, or tasks, of communication within the notions, or content categories, of instruction. In *¡Hola!*, *¿Qué tal?*, and *¡Adelante!*, activities are often based on language functions such as gathering information, reporting, and expressing preferences and opinions. These simplified language functions tie in closely with the topical and structural content of the unit in which they are practiced. Students who participate in these activities are building the skills to perform concrete language functions within meaningful contexts. That is, they are acquiring the skills to perform communication tasks that naturally relate to their immediate world and interests.

As a result, the language functions and notions are consistent with the program's emphasis on meaningful and comprehensible communication that evolves naturally as students progress in their acquisition of a second language. |
| **Experience—Using What Works Best** | In summary, the methodologies, approaches, and techniques incorporated in the *¡Viva el español!* program have all been tempered by the practical, commonsense knowledge that has evolved during the many collective years of classroom and materials-development experience of the program's authors, contributors, and consultants. It is expected—and even hoped—that you will pick and choose from the suggestions and examples contained in this *Annotated Teacher's Edition* to tailor your Spanish-language program to the ages, backgrounds, needs, and abilities of your students. Young children and early adolescents will communicate to you whether a certain approach is working. The keys to a successful, stimulating language-learning environment are to use only what works and to inject variety and fun, mixed with the occasional surprise, into your classroom routine. |

Components of the *¡Viva el español!* Textbook Series

| **Annotated Teacher's Edition** | The teacher's editions of *¡Hola!*, *¿Qué tal?*, and *¡Adelante!* form the core of the program. In each *Annotated Teacher's Edition* (A.T.E.), you can find the information you will need to plan and implement a course of study over the school year, adapt the program to meet the unique needs of your students, carry out the daily lessons, enrich the language-learning experience, assess students' progress, and integrate the school's Spanish program |

into the home and community. The A.T.E. also contains a full-size reproduction of the student textbook with annotations for information, suggestions for extending and enriching the daily lessons, and the answers to exercises.

In the front section of the *Annotated Teacher's Edition*, you will find a discussion of the features and methodologies of the *¡Viva el español!* program; a complete scope and sequence chart containing the unit-by-unit active vocabulary, points of grammar and language usage, and language skills, functions, and cultural topics; unit-by-unit plans, listing the materials and components you will need; suggestions for review, extension, enrichment, and informal assessment activities; a resource section of games and activities; and a reproduction of the ACTFL Proficiency Guidelines for the Novice and Intermediate levels.

Textbooks

The colorful student textbooks contain an introductory unit, 10–12 regular units, useful appendixes for reference, a Spanish-English word list, an English-Spanish word list, and a general index. From the beginning of the school year, students should learn to use all the features of the textbook as tools in building their language skills. (The organization of the textbook will be described later in detail.)

Resource and Activity Book

The blackline masters in the *Resource and Activity Book* contain numerous black-and-white illustrations to enhance classroom activities and to save you time in searching for and preparing materials for the classroom. Each book of blackline masters is divided into eight sections:

1. *¡Hablemos!* masters, which reproduce in black and white the vocabulary section art of each regular unit of the textbook

2. Vocabulary Cards masters, which provide individual illustrations of the vocabulary for use in TPR activities, games, etc.

3. Vocabulary Review masters, which are reduced illustrations of vocabulary groups on a single page

4. *¡A conversar!* masters, which are extended dialogues or readings that incorporate language from the units

5. Numbers/Letters masters, which allow you to review or reteach numbers and letters

6. Maps, which are outline maps for extension and enrichment activities

7. Game/Activity Pages

8. Tape Exercise and Pronunciation Pages, which are the written exercises that accompany the Exercise Cassette and pronunciation explanations and exercises

In addition, a complete answer key to the Tape Exercise and Pronunciation Pages is printed in the front of the *Resource and Activity Book*. You will also find a complete tapescript of the Lesson Cassettes and Exercise Cassettes, as well as the music and lyrics of the songs recorded on the Song Cassette. The tapescript is designed to help you select the conversations and features of the audiocassettes that will enrich the listening comprehension experiences of your students.

Workbook

Each student workbook is correlated to the textbook units. Included in the workbooks are exercises to practice writing skills, reinforce the vocabulary and language concepts taught in the textbook, develop language-learning skills, and have fun with the language. As in the textbook, the activities and exercises in the workbook are provided at three levels of difficulty to meet the needs of students' learning styles and abilities.

Workbook— Teacher's Edition

The *Teacher's Edition* of the workbook contains the answers to the exercises. It also includes the symbols that represent the level of the exercises, and suggestions for using and extending exercises.

Audiocassettes

The audiocassettes that accompany the *¡Viva el español!* textbook series fall into four categories:

1. Lesson Cassettes

2. Exercise Cassettes

3. Song Cassette

4. Test Cassette

Lesson Cassettes

Recorded by native speakers of Spanish of varied ages and backgrounds, the Lesson Cassettes contain the vocabulary sections of each regular unit of the textbook as well as selected other material.

The Lesson Cassettes also contain conversations and features to provide students with additional opportunities to hear the language spoken by native speakers in simulated real-life situations. The conversations and features not only synthesize the vocabulary and structures of each unit, but also serve as practical examples of the language in use.

Exercise Cassettes	The Exercise Cassettes contain exercises that further students' practice in distinguishing sounds and in using the structures of the language. Some of the exercises have been designed for oral responses and others have been designed for paper-and-pencil responses on the Tape Exercise and Pronunciation Pages found in the *Resource and Activity Book*.
Song Cassette	The Song Cassette contains all the songs that are included in the *Resource and Activity Book*.
Test Cassette	The Test Cassette accompanies the **¡Viva el español!** *Testing Program*, which is described below.
Testing	The Testing Program for **¡Hola!**, **¿Qué tal?**, and **¡Adelante!** is made up of a blackline master book of tests and a Test Cassette. Not only does the blackline master book contain all the tests you will need throughout the school year, it also provides a student progress chart for you to record each student's development of language proficiencies, a complete discussion of strategies for assessing and evaluating students' abilities and, of course, an answer key. Recorded on the Test Cassette are listening comprehension activities that correspond to the *Testing Program*.
Overhead Transparencies	Full-color overhead transparencies at each level of the textbook series reproduce all *¡Hablemos!* art without labels. These transparencies can prove invaluable in initial presentation of vocabulary, in cuing for extending practice, and in TPR activities.
Culture Resource Book	These 80-page blackline master books provide you with rich cultural activities and information to reproduce and share with students across the year. Each book also contains maps and facts on different Spanish-speaking countries.

Special Features of the *Annotated Teacher's Edition*

Throughout the Unit Plan section of this *Annotated Teacher's Edition*, and in the on-page annotations, you will find countless suggestions for strategies and ideas for enriching your teaching and your students' learning experience. Following is a listing of the types of suggestions you will find, with an explanation of their content.

Presentation Suggestions

These notes offer you ideas for presenting new words or structures, for setting up activities, or for otherwise preparing students for understanding new material or tasks.

Culture: Photos and Realia

Cultural photos and authentic realia in the program are explained. Much of this information can be shared with students, or can be used for your background information. In many cases, the notes provide ideas for communicative questions or activities that can work with the images.

The Multi-level Class

These are suggestions for dealing with the special needs of your students, whether they are struggling with the concepts and require different modes of presentation and practice, or are excelling and need extra challenges and enrichment.

The Heritage Speaker

Many teachers find that they have students in their classes who already speak Spanish by way of heritage, or for whom Spanish is the dominant language. This feature will give you ideas for meeting the needs of Spanish-speaking students in the Spanish classroom, including suggestions for challenging activities, extension of practice that will involve their knowledge of their cultures of origin or will formalize their linguistic knowledge, ways of involving them in cooperative learning tasks, and suggestions for using the special resources that they bring to your class.

Assessment Opportunities

Here you will find ideas for informal and formal assessment, frequently working from the activities and other resources in the Student Textbook. Suggestions include ways of assessing communicative proficiency, as well as achievement and prochievement. Ideas for creating portfolios, notebooks, drawings, and other tangible products for assessment are also given.

Language Across the Curriculum

These are ideas for integrating content area material into the language class, or, conversely, integrating language into content areas, including, but not limited to, social studies, math, science, geography, language arts, music, and art.

Enrichment

It is important to go beyond the student page, occasionally, to bring in additional related language and to challenge students to see a larger context for what they are learning. These suggestions will help you do that.

Extension

These are ideas for extending the practice begun in student exercises or activities, either by adding items from other sources, redoing an exercise with a different pattern, or moving a mechanical- or meaningful-level exercise into the communicative realm.

Listening Comprehension

Students will benefit from practice in which they listen to pick out meaning from longer utterances, or to determine differences in meaning between similar sounding words, etc. These sections will give you ideas for focusing students' attention on sound and meaning, isolating the listening skill so that students are not being asked to write or speak, but simply to demonstrate understanding.

Cooperative Learning

These are hints for setting up practice in which students can work cooperatively to perform a task or help one another understand new material. Also included are ideas for pairing students so that heritage speakers and advanced students can serve as resources for slower students.

Re-enter/Recycle

Because the *¡Viva el español!* program is designed for constant spiraling and re-entry of previously taught material, there are frequent opportunities to reteach or review with students things that they've learned before. These opportunities are highlighted in this feature.

Tap Background Knowledge

At the beginning of each Unit Plan you will find ideas for activating students' prior knowledge of a topic so that they will better be able to make connections with what they are about to learn.

TPR

This feature offers tips for integrating TPR into your teaching and provides model sentences and new commands to use in TPR activities.

Critical Thinking

Language learning offers wonderful possibilities for developing critical or higher-order thinking skills. Throughout the program, you will find suggestions for developing these important abilities in your students, using the material at hand.

For the Nonspecialist

Because we recognize that a number of teachers teaching Spanish at the elementary and middle-school levels are not necessarily specialists in language teaching or in the Spanish language, we've offered many helpful suggestions that will provide necessary background information, and make life simpler for these teachers.

How to Use and Teach the
¡Viva el Español!
Textbook Series

¡Viva el español! is a complete, integrated series that will help you meet the needs of all your students, no matter what your curriculum, and no matter what your teaching style. The following sections will provide helpful information about the organization of the series and of the textbooks, describe the purposes and uses of each section and subsection, offer ideas for general strategies and techniques, give recommendations for structuring and pacing your lessons, and tell you how the various components of the series work together to create an exciting, effective language-learning program.

Organization of the Textbooks: Preliminary Lessons

Each of the textbooks begins with a preliminary unit. In *¡Hola!* this unit is called **¡Bienvenidos!** In *¿Qué tal?* and *¡Adelante!* there is an **Unidad de repaso** to start the year.

In *¡Hola!*, the first textbook in the series, the **¡Bienvenidos!** unit begins with basic communication practice involving greetings, numbers, and classroom vocabulary. The unit is divided into three separate lessons. Throughout these lessons, beginning students are eased into second-language learning through high-frequency practice, success-oriented vocabulary, and strategies to help them not only learn language, but also begin to learn how to learn a language. Each lesson begins with *¡Hablemos!* (discussed below) and extensive practice. If students are coming into your program with prior experience in speaking Spanish—either from having studied with the *¡Viva el español! Learning Systems A, B,* and *C,* or because they are heritage speakers of the language—the **¡Bienvenidos!** unit can serve as an opportunity to review familiar language and learn some new words and expressions.

In the second and third textbooks in the series, *¿Qué tal?* and *¡Adelante!*, the preliminary **Unidad de repaso** provides an opportunity for review and reteaching. The practice in these sections serves as a reminder and refresher to reaccustom students to Spanish after the summer break. The situational practice and activities cover all the important vocabulary and communication concepts from the previous book.

Organization of the Textbooks: Regular Units

After the preliminary units, the units in each book follow a regular pattern that will help you pace and plan your teaching, and that will offer your students the additional support of knowing what to expect and where to look to find information. *¡Hola!* contains ten regular units, while *¿Qué tal?* and *¡Adelante!* have twelve units each. The sections of each unit are described here in terms of general content and purposes. Throughout the Unit Plans section of this *Annotated Teacher's Edition*, and in the on-page annotations, you will find extensive help and suggestions for teaching each section of the units.

Unit Opener

Every unit throughout the program begins with a colorful opener on a two-page spread that can be introduced on the first day of a new unit or on the testing day of the prior unit. On the left-hand page of each unit opener, you will find a title that sets the communication theme of the unit. Just below that is a paragraph in large, colored type that seeks to activate students' prior knowledge of the topic and engage them in what is to come. Following that is a list of learning and communication objectives written in language students can easily understand. The Unit Plan notes will give you ideas for tapping background knowledge and moving students into the unit.

The right-hand page features colorful photographs from around the Spanish-speaking world that are linked to the communication and culture themes of the unit. The captions often foreshadow the language to be introduced, providing a source of comprehensible input. Culture notes in the Unit Plan section or in on-page annotations will give you background information on those photos that call for extra explanation, as well as offering you ideas for using the photos for communication practice and recycling of previously taught material.

You will also find here the *¿Sabes que...?* features. These are collections of short, interesting cultural facts that you can share with your students or that they can read on their own. The information is designed both to compare and contrast cultures, sensitizing students to see both what is different and what is the same across cultures. The *¿Sabes que...?* features are linked to the general themes of the unit.

¡Hablemos!

The *¡Hablemos!* sections provide the basic communication models and vocabulary that will be used throughout the unit. There are two *¡Hablemos!* sections in each unit, each presenting an average of six to eight new words or expressions that are linked to one another lexically or thematically. Research and experience indicate that this is the most effective method of fostering vocabulary retention.

Every *¡Hablemos!* has one or two brief communication models followed by illustrations that present new vocabulary. The models and illustration labels are not translated into English on these pages. This helps students more directly establish links between meaning and the Spanish word, rather than resorting to translation. The illustrations serve almost as icons representing the words. The full-color overhead transparencies available with the program will allow you to focus all your students' attention on the picture you want them to look at, and will be useful in cuing in extended practice.

The communication models are designed to allow you to substitute the pictured vocabulary in various slots in the conversations. By introducing the model first, and then substituting the pictured vocabulary, you can give a more interesting and meaningful initial presentation than if you were simply to point to a picture and say, **Es el lápiz.** The conversation models lend themselves beautifully to getting students to simulate real interchanges. Because they are brief and easily modified, the conversations can be performed by several pairs of students without becoming tedious.

The *Así es...* boxes that appear in many of the *¡Hablemos!* sections provide paragraphs of additional cultural information on single topics. In many cases they are accompanied by related photos and by additional cultural information in the teacher annotations.

Practiquemos

¡Hablemos! is followed immediately by a set of practice activities that will allow students to begin using the language in context. Practice in *¡Viva el español!* is rich and varied. Exercises are set in meaningful and realistic

contexts so that students understand the communicative purpose of what they're learning. The variety of practice will help you meet the needs of all your students with their various learning styles.

There is a general progression of practice from more mechanical (with single right answers), to meaningful (where students are providing some information, but still within fairly strict limits), to communicative (more open-ended practice, where students are answering in creative ways about real information). In the *Teacher's Edition*, these levels are indicated beside each exercise or activity with the following symbols:

○ Mechanical

◐ Meaningful

● Communicative

You will also see icons that tell you whether a practice is intended for pair work or small group work:

Pair work

Group work

The instructions for exercises and activities have been kept flexible so that you may change the intent of a particular practice. For example, you might choose to assign an essentially oral exercise as written practice. You may also wish to extend a mechanical or meaningful exercise to the next level of practice, making it meaningful or communicative. The Unit Plans and on-page annotations will give you countless ideas for doing this, as well as for tailoring practice to the needs of slower students, advanced students, or heritage speakers. The notes will help you with set-up and presentation of exercises, as well as giving you the answers for those that have answers.

Entre amigos

Each sequence of practice throughout the program ends with an *Entre amigos* activity. These are all at either the meaningful or communicative level, and are always designed for pair or group practice. Some provide high-interest extended reading practice. Others provide writing practice. Many are styled as games. Some call for materials such as index cards, paper bags, art supplies, pictures from magazines, etc. These will always be listed in the Unit Plans section under "Materials to Gather" so that you can prepare in advance. The notes also give ideas for setting up, extending, or enriching the activities.

In many instances, the *Entre amigos* activities lend themselves to Language Across the Curriculum practice, calling on students to integrate skills from math, language arts, social studies, geography, art, and other content areas. These activities will prove extremely rewarding both for you and your students as you see the immediate communicative applications of the language being learned.

¿Cómo lo dices?   Communicative functions and language structures are explained in two or three sections in each unit called *¿Cómo lo dices?* Each begins with an objective, stated either as a communicative function or a question, that indicates to students what communicative purpose is served by the language being discussed. Inductive methods of instruction are used frequently, whereby students are asked to build their own understanding of the structure based on guided observation of examples of language in use. Extensive illustrations give visual learners extra assistance in grasping the meaning of the material. Suggestions for presentation and for TPR activities are given in the Unit Plans and in the on-page annotations.

Throughout the program, you should avoid teaching grammar for grammar's sake. What is important is that students learn to use language, not that they learn to state its rules or describe it. All humans who use language have an innate understanding that there is an underlying structure to the way a language is put together, and will seek to ferret out what that order is. However, being able to *describe* the order is not necessarily the same as being able to *function* within that order. We have avoided using traditional grammatical terminology as much as possible. Students will be more successful if they understand what they have to do to be understood, rather than if they can rattle off the endings of a particular verb group.

Integrating actual practice of structures with your presentation of structures is probably the most effective means of leading students to proficiency. You might even want to have students do the practice exercises *before* you spend time explaining the underlying structure. This requires more effort on your part in leading students through the exercises, but may well pay off in increased proficiency.

¡Úsalo!   *¿Cómo lo dices?* has its own sequence of practice exercises and activities called *¡Úsalo!* The title of the section describes its purpose: getting students to use the language. In most cases, you will find two to four exercises for each structural discussion, ending with an *Entre amigos* activity. See the discussions of the *Practiquemos* and *Entre amigos* activities above for an explanation of the kinds of practice you will find in the *¡Úsalo!* sections, as well as the resources available to help you in working with students on these activities.

¡A divertirnos!   These end-of-unit activities are just what the title says: fun! Whether students are playing a game, learning a song, making a piñata, building a diorama, or whipping up a batch of *huevos a la mexicana*, they will be rewarded by these entertaining, integrative activities that build on communication skills or enrich the cultural understanding of your students. Necessary materials are highlighted in the "Materials to Gather" list in the Unit Plans, and extensive suggestions for presentation, extension, and enrichment are provided as well.

Photos and Realia   Throughout the program, you will find hundreds of colorful photos and numerous realia pieces from around the Spanish-speaking world. The photos have been selected to complement and enrich the themes of each unit, while providing a cultural context for learning. In addition, they offer you excellent opportunities for communication practice, whether as the basis for a series of questions, or as a springboard for a comprehensible input narrative. The notes and annotations will give you important background where necessary, and make suggestions for extension or activities based on the photos. You may want to use the photos as the launching pad for your own cultural presentations and activities.

Using the Components of the *¡Viva el español!* Textbook Series

The student texts and *Annotated Teacher's Editions* of *¡Viva el español!* are designed to be stand-alone, self-sufficient books that give you the basis for your curriculum. Of course, there are excellent supplemental components that can enrich your teaching and give you additional resources for the classroom. (For a complete listing and description of additional components, see the article on p. T-18.) Each unit of the program is designed to be taught over approximately fourteen days, including time for bringing in enrichment activities and other resources. You may extend or shorten the time as needed, depending on the length of your class periods as well as on the learning styles and abilities of your students. The chart on the following pages will help you see how to pace your teaching and integrate all of the various supplemental components in your planning.

¡Viva el Español!
Planning and Pacing Chart

Unit Sections	Day 1	Day 2	Day 3	Day 4	Day 5	Day 6	Day 7
Introduction and *¿Sabes que...?*	Present **ST, RB**						
¡Hablemos! and *Así es...*	Present **ST, RB, OH**	Present **ST, RB, OH**	Review **T, W**	Review **T, W**	Informal Assessment		
Practiquemos and *Entre amigos*			Practice **ST, W**				
¡Hablemos! and *Así es...*				Present **ST, RB, OH**	Present **ST, RB, OH**	Review **T**	
Practiquemos and *Entre amigos*					Practice **ST, RB**	Practice **ST, RB**	
¿Cómo lo dices?						Present **ST, ATE**	Present **ST, ATE**
¡Úsalo! and *Entre amigos*						Practice **ST, ATE, W, RB**	Practice **ST, ATE, W, RB**
¿Cómo lo dices?							
¡Úsalo! and *Entre amigos*							
¡A divertirnos!							
Review activities	Warm-up **ATE**	Warm-up **ATE**	Warm-up **ATE**	Warm-up **ATE**	Warm-up **ATE**	Warm-up **ATE**	Warm-up **ATE**
Extension and enrichment activities	**ATE, SC (RB, W)**	**ATE, SC (RB, W)**	**ATE, SC (CB)**	**ATE, SC (CB)**	**ATE (RB, W)**	**ATE (RB, W)**	**ATE, SC (CB)**

Abbreviations

ATE	Annotated Teacher's Edition	LC	Lesson Cassette
ST	Student Textbook	EC	Exercise Cassette
W	Workbook	SC	Song Cassette
RB	Resource and Activity Book	T	Testing Program
CB	Culture Resource Book	TC	Test Cassette
		OH	Overhead Transparencies

Day 8	Day 9	Day 10	Day 11	Day 12	Day 13	Day 14
				Informal Assessment	Review **T**	Test **T, TC**
Informal Assessment	Review				Review **T**	Test **T, TC**
Practice **ST, ATE, RB, W**						
	Present **ST, ATE**	Present **ST, ATE**	Informal Assessment	Review **W, OH**	Review **T**	Test **T, TC**
Practice	Practice **ST, ATE RB, W**	Practice **ST, ATE RB, W**				
			Present **ST, ATE**	Present **ST, ATE**		
Warm-up **ATE**	Warm-up **ATE**	Warm-up **ATE**	Warm-up **ATE**	Warm-up **ATE**	Warm-up **ATE**	Warm-up **ATE**
ATE, SC (RB, W)	**ATE, SC (RB, W)**	**ATE, SC (CB)**	**ATE, SC (CB)**	**ATE (RB, W)**	**ATE (RB, W)**	**ATE, SC**

General Strategies and Techniques

In this section you will find numerous suggestions for strategies and techniques to use in the *¡Viva el español!* language classroom. Different techniques and strategies may result in success at different stages of the learning process. Whichever suggestions you follow, it is wise to keep the following points in mind:

- Allow students to respond spontaneously. Requiring them to speak before they are ready may produce anxiety and actually impede their progress.

- If a strategy is successful, add it to the many strategies you use in the classroom. Adapt it, vary it, and enrich it; however, do not use it exclusively. Even the tastiest dishes become boring if they are the mainstay of your diet.

- If a strategy is not successful, drop it. What works well with one group of students may not work at all with another group.

- Be sensitive to the emotional, as well as the cognitive, needs of your students. Very young students are often willing to engage in whimsical activities, whereas self-conscious early adolescents may not do something that they perceive as foolish or silly.

- Provide continual constructive, positive feedback. The most satisfying reaction is one which indicates you have understood the *message*, of what the student is trying to convey—particularly if you respond just as you would in normal communication. Positive reinforcement may also consist of a nod and a smile, a pat on the back, or an enthusiastic **¡Muy bien!** Students should be rewarded for doing their personal best as well as achieving a standard of linguistic accuracy.

◆ Use props, costumes, realia, and puppets in the classroom. Even older students sometimes find it easier to speak through a puppet or to assume a character role because attention is then diverted from themselves. Especially during the awkward, vulnerable early teenage years, students may need the comfort of a psychological security blanket when learning something new.

Suggestions for Teaching Vocabulary

Setting the Stage for TPR

Total Physical Response (TPR) methods have proven to be effective in teaching vocabulary. Teachers who have used TPR in the classroom report extreme satisfaction with the results: students remember the vocabulary over long periods of time. In fact, with little prompting, students have recalled vocabulary quickly even after the summer vacation break. In a beginning class, you may wish to devote the first class periods of the school year to teaching the TPR commands themselves before the textbooks are distributed. During the school year, you may incorporate new commands into the daily lessons and combine commands in new ways to add variety and stimulate interest.

As early as the first day of class, you can teach some useful commands for TPR activities as well as classroom management. You may wish to begin by explaining that you will give yourself a command and that you will then carry out that command. The following sequence is recommended for presenting and modeling new commands:

1. Give yourself the command and then act it out. Repeat the procedure at least three times.

2. Give the command and act it out, with the entire class following along.

3. Give the command but do not act it out. Students respond on their own.

4. Give the command to small groups and individuals.

5. Have students volunteer to give the command to you and the class.

6. Have students give the command to one another in pairs or small groups.

Steps 5 and 6 may be carried out after students have exhibited willingness to speak and are ready to work independently. Students who have participated in the *¡Viva el español! Learning Systems A, B,* and *C* may make willing volunteers for the initial small-group activities.

Later in the process, you may expand on the TPR commands by giving them in writing. To prepare students for reading commands, you may write the command on the chalkboard and point to it before following steps 1 through 3 of the TPR sequence. Then, volunteers may point to a command, say it aloud, and have the class respond appropriately.

Preparing to Teach Vocabulary

Each regular unit of *¡Hola!*, *¿Qué tal?*, and *¡Adelante!* begins with the *¡Hablemos!* vocabulary section. These sections are reproduced in the *Resource and Activity Book* (blackline masters) and on the full-color Overhead Transparencies. For the initial presentation of vocabulary, these blackline master pages may also be made into transparencies for use on the overhead projector or be enlarged on a photocopier and mounted for use as flash cards. Also included in the Vocabulary Cards section of the *Resource* book are illustrations of the individual vocabulary words. These illustrations may be duplicated, mounted on heavy-gauge paper, and then laminated to become a classroom set of vocabulary cards. The effort expended in preparing these materials will be rewarded, as you will soon have a permanent set of classroom materials that will last for years. The illustrations may also be photocopied and distributed to students, allowing them to compile their own sets of vocabulary cards throughout the year.

Presenting the Vocabulary

Armed with the Overhead Transparencies or other illustrations, you are ready to begin teaching vocabulary. It is recommended that an average of four to eight vocabulary words be taught during one class period. Depending on your particular class, the number of words may range from a minimum of three to a maximum of eight. In general, the following procedure may be used for presenting, modeling, and practicing new vocabulary:

1. Point to, touch, or hold up an illustration of the word (if practical, use the real object), and say the word. Repeat this step at least three times (e.g., **La ventana. La ventana. Es la ventana. Ésta es la ventana.**).

2. Demonstrate the word as it is used in the mini-conversation in the *¡Hablemos!* section. Model the conversation yourself, then involve a student with you.

3. Continue by asking a question to which students may respond either nonverbally or verbally. Repeat this several times, as in the following examples:

   Yes/no questions

   > **T:** (*pointing to or touching the window*) **¿Es la ventana? ¿Sí o no? ¿Es la ventana?**

   > **S: Sí.** (Students may also respond by nodding their heads.)

   Either-or questions

   > **T:** (*pointing to or touching the window*) **¿Es la ventana o es la puerta? ¿Es la ventana o es la puerta?**

   > **S: La ventana.** (*or*) **Es la ventana.**

4. Practice the vocabulary by using vocabulary cards and giving TPR commands, such as the following:

   > **T:** *Anita,* **anda con la ventana.**

   > *Diego,* **pásale la ventana a** *Rita.*

   > *Inés,* **pon la ventana en mi escritorio.**

   > *Susana,* **dibuja una ventana en la pizarra.**

   > *Eduardo,* **borra la ventana.**

   > *Juan,* **salta con la ventana. Dale la ventana a** *Ricardo.*

   > *Alumnos,* **brinquen con la ventana.**

5. After students have demonstrated their comprehension of the words, volunteers may take turns giving commands to the class, or students may work in small groups or pairs to practice the vocabulary or model the conversations.

Useful Commands for TPR Activities and Classroom Exercises

abre / abran (open)

anda / anden (walk)

asómate / asómense (look out of)

borra / borren (erase)

brinca / brinquen (jump)

busca / busquen (look for)

canta / canten (sing)

cierra / cierren (close)

colorea / coloreen (color)

contesta / contesten (answer)

corta / corten (cut)

cuenta / cuenten (count)

da / den (give)

da / den un saltito (hop)

date / dense una vuelta (turn around)

di / digan (say)

dibuja / dibujen (draw)

dobla / doblen (fold; turn)

entra / entren (enter)

escoge / escojan (choose)

escribe / escriban (write)

escucha / escuchen (listen)

habla / hablen (talk)

levanta / levanten la mano
(raise your hand)

levántate / levántense (stand up)

mira / miren (look)

muestra / muestren (show)

párate / párense (stand up; stop)

pasa / pasen (pass)

pon / pongan (put)

pregunta / pregunten (ask)

quita / quiten (take off)

recoge / recojan (pick up)

recorta / recorten (cut out)

repite / repitan (repeat)

responde / respondan (respond)

saca / saquen (take out)

sal / salgan (leave)

salta / salten (jump)

señala / señalen (point to)

siéntate / siéntense (sit down)

sigue / sigan (follow)

suma / sumen (add up)

tira / tiren (throw)

toca / toquen (touch)

toma / tomen (take)

trae / traigan (bring)

ve / vayan (go)

ven / vengan (come)

As students progress throughout the **¡*Viva el español!*** textbook series, you may increase the amount of comprehensible input with each unit by incorporating previously learned vocabulary and structures into the presentation of new vocabulary. For example, when presenting the **tener** expression, **tengo calor**, you may combine the previously learned weather expressions with pantomiming techniques:

> **T:** *(fanning yourself and wiping your forehead)* **No hace viento. No hace frío. Hace calor. Hace mucho calor.** *(pointing to yourself)* **Tengo calor. Tengo calor. Tengo mucho calor.**

By increasing comprehensible input, you help students to sharpen their listening skills and to derive meaning from context.

Suggestions for Teaching Structures

Inductive Approach

In **¡*Hola!*, ¿*Qué tal?*,** and **¡*Adelante!*,** the inductive approach has been used frequently to teach language usage and structures. With this approach, students first hear, see, and read specific examples of a point of grammar and then form a general conclusion about it. For example, in the *¿Cómo lo dices?* sections of each regular unit, students see illustrated examples of a part of speech, such as subject pronouns. First they look at the pictures, hear and/or read the words below the pictures, and then answer questions about what they have observed. Following this, they practice with examples of the part of speech used in context—usually through questions and answers. From their observations and practice with examples in context, students—under your guidance—draw conclusions or form simply stated rules about how that part of the language works.

When you present a new structure, supplement the presentation with as much comprehensible input as possible before students even open their textbooks. That is, begin the presentation with oral examples of the language structure. For example, when introducing **estudiar** with **-ar** verbs, pantomime or act out the activity while you talk to the students:

> **T:** *(pantomiming)* **Estudio mucho. Estudio en casa. Estudio en la escuela. También estudio en la biblioteca. No estudio mucho los domingos. Pero sí estudio los lunes, los martes, los miércoles, los jueves y los viernes.**

By demonstrating a structure, you give students the opportunity to hear it used in context before they see it in writing. Also, by including familiar vocabulary and structures, students can experience the language passively with comprehension before they use it actively themselves.

After students have been exposed to the language structure, they are ready to begin forming conclusions about it. In the textbooks, have students observe the illustrations as you read the words or sentences below them aloud. Point out features in the illustrations that help convey the meanings of the words. Guide students in answering the questions posed in the text. After students have completed the presentation and have read or heard the examples of the structure in context, help them come to a conclusion about the language. By stating a rule of language in their own words, students are more likely to remember it. Once stated, these rules are to be remembered but not memorized and recited.

At the beginning of each *¿Cómo lo dices?* presentation, you will find a description of the communicative intent of the section. These have been worded very simply, as they might actually be stated by the students themselves. These simplified statements help avoid the excessive use of grammatical terminology. Students at this stage of their education may not know the parts of speech and the grammatical terms as they apply to their first language. Therefore, reliance on prior knowledge of grammar and terms has been avoided.

Grammatical terms are introduced and defined as needed throughout the textbooks. Students should be aware of these terms, but they should not be expected to memorize them or define them as part of the assessment of their progress. It is more important that they incorporate the newly acquired information in their everyday communication than it is that they recite a rule or conjugate a verb.

Techniques of inductive learning are not equally successful with all students. If your students demonstrate frustration with not being able to understand what is expected of them, you may wish to try a different approach. For example, you may reverse the process. That is, you may begin with the general statement about the language and follow up with specific examples of its use. In practical terms, you may present the rule first, encouraging students to repeat it or read it aloud. Or you may write the rule on the chalkboard and encourage students to write it in their notebooks. Then, from the rule you may progress to its application, as given in the illustrated examples, charts, and contextual examples of its use in the textbook. It is more important to develop communication and maintain a low-stress learning environment than it is to adhere to a specific technique of instruction.

If students have difficulty with a particular concept, do not spend an inordinate amount of time trying to explain it. The language is continually reinforced and reintroduced throughout the textbook series. For example, the singular forms of regular **-ar**, **-er**, and **-ir** verbs are presented and practiced in *¡Hola!* They are reintroduced and reinforced in *¿Qué tal?* when students learn the plural forms of the verbs.

Suggestions for Developing Reading Skills

The spectrum of reading skills in young students may not be fully developed in their first language. Therefore, you may find yourself teaching some of the basic skills of reading as well as teaching reading skills in the second language. However, any approach to reading begins simply and develops gradually.

Reading as Support for Speaking and Listening

Beginning students have some very basic needs in order to become acquainted with the written language. Familiarity or awareness of accent marks, punctuation, and sound-letter correspondences can begin early on. Just as children begin to develop reading skills by being read to while looking at the text of a book, beginning language students may also begin their reading development by associating sounds with their written equivalents. In short, reading begins as a support for speaking and listening skills.

Reading skills may develop from reading isolated words to reading complete sentences. You may start, for example, by having a student match word cards to vocabulary cards. Word cards may be made from 3″ x 5″ index cards with the word printed neatly on one side. These cards may then be used to match the written word to its vocabulary-card illustration, which is provided in the *Resource and Activity Book*. This activity of passive reading is nonthreatening and parallels the acquisition of reading skills in the first language.

Gradually, in the security of a group, students may read the words aloud in choral reading activities as a class and in smaller groups, such as by rows. Then after they have practiced, you may ask volunteers to read the words aloud. As with speaking, individuals should read aloud only when they are ready. Following this approach, students may progress to reading the words in context and finally to reading complete sentences based on familiar material.

Once the sounds of the language have been related to the written forms of the language, you can begin to develop more sophisticated skills, such as guessing the meanings of unfamiliar words from visual and textual contexts and deriving meanings by recognizing cognates. Throughout the annotated pages of the student textbooks and in the specific Unit Plans in the front of the *Annotated Teacher's Edition*, you will find many practical suggestions for helping students to develop these skills.

Basic Reading Skills

Reading skills in Spanish may then progress to the broader, basic reading skills of skimming, scanning, reading for specific information, and reading for general meaning. It is important for students to realize that they do not have to understand every single word in a passage or simulated document in order to understand its general meaning.

Skimming

The reading skill of skimming—a quick, overall glance at a passage or selection—helps students understand the framework of the selection. For example, students may quickly skim a selection to determine that it is an advertisement, a questionnaire, a friendly letter, or a conversation between two people. Once they identify the framework, they consciously or subconsciously trigger information they have stored about that framework in their own language.

Scanning

Scanning, another reading skill, involves looking for specific pieces of information. For example, students may scan a friendly letter to find out who wrote it or they may scan a television schedule to find a particular program.

Students can incorporate these skills in their second-language reading by following your guidance. For example, before beginning to read a selection, you may ask students to state what the selection is. The reading activities in the *Entre amigos* sections of the textbooks often lend themselves to practice in skimming and scanning.

Reading for Information

Reading for specific information may first involve scanning the selection to locate the information and then reading every word to understand the information itself. For example, in answering questions following a passage in an *Entre amigos* section, students may practice scanning the passage to find key words and then reading the sentence or sentences carefully to find the information they need to answer the questions. As students progress in their language studies and as their reading encompasses Spanish-language materials (newspapers, novels, magazines, and works of nonfiction), the skills of skimming, scanning, and reading for information that have been developed in their early studies will become increasingly valuable to them.

Reading for General Meaning

The skill of reading to understand the gist of a passage or selection most closely approximates the reading people do for pleasure. In this kind of reading, it is not necessary to understand every word nor to process the information for a specific purpose. Instead, it is more useful to comprehend the overall meaning as it advances the plot or relates to the character. Only when the student experiences difficulty in grasping that meaning is it necessary to isolate the barriers to understanding and then to solve the problem by looking up the troublesome words or expressions in the dictionary. At the beginning stages of reading, students may read a selection first for general meaning; for example, they may begin by quickly reading a friendly letter as part of an *Entre amigos* activity. Then, as students answer the questions in the friendly letter or formulate their own questions for their "pen pal," they may read the letter again for specific information.

In many instances, you may discover that the basic skills of skimming, scanning, reading for specific information, and reading for general meaning have not been acquired in the first language. You may then need to provide practice in developing the skills themselves in addition to applying those skills to reading selections in Spanish. Although time in the classroom is short, it is important to address the need to develop solid, basic reading skills in your students if they are to progress successfully from reading carefully controlled selections to reading lengthier, richer, authentic materials in the Spanish language.

The path is easier, of course, if students recognize that a skill they have practiced in a language arts class can be applied to their activities in Spanish class. At the beginning of the school year, you may wish to work together with the language arts teachers to determine the kinds of skills that can be applied in the second-language classroom as well as to exchange practical ideas for teaching and reinforcing those skills.

Suggestions for Teaching Writing Skills

The development of writing skills in the target language is similar to the development of reading skills. As students progress in writing, they may begin with isolated words, develop with complete sentences, and then flourish with directed or original compositions.

Beginning with Individual Words

Writing skills may begin in conjunction with learning new vocabulary. Once comprehension of the spoken word has been established, you may then combine reading and writing skills development. The following procedure is recommended for initial writing skills development.

1. Write the word (or words) on the chalkboard or on a transparency for the overhead projector.

2. Pronounce one word at a time and have the class repeat it.

3. Spell the word and have the class repeat it.

4. Spell the word and have the class write it.

Four to eight words is the most you should use in initial writing practice. In the beginning, writing skills and speaking skills are closely linked. At first, students may copy or write words and sentences they have only practiced orally. In this way, writing is a controlled skill that depends on and reinforces speaking skills. Many of the exercises provided in *¡Hola!*, *¿Qué tal?*, and *¡Adelante!* may first be completed orally in class and then used as writing practice to support students' speaking abilities. Likewise, Language Experience Approach activities, such as producing Big Books, also reinforce speaking activities. These are controlled activities, yet they give students the sense that they are writing and creating their own materials.

Applying the Writing Process

As students develop in their first language, they learn that writing is a process. Initially they learn and practice skills of choosing a topic, identifying their audience, gathering information, and organizing the information. These activities form the prewriting process.

Once these skills have been practiced, students move on to the writing process itself. They develop their ideas by writing the information in a non-critical first draft, followed by a "cooling-off" period. Then they revise the first draft by reading it critically and by changing sentences and paragraphs according to the organization of their topic and the clarity of meaning of their paragraphs. They read the revised draft again to edit it, correcting errors they recognize such as misspelled words, incorrect subject-verb agreement, etc. The final step in the process is the preparation of a clean copy of their writing and a final proofreading to ensure that the text is as good as they can make it.

If students are just beginning to learn and practice these skills in their first language, it is unrealistic to expect them to produce error-free compositions in their second language. Although it is not necessary to focus on the writing process in the second-language classroom, it is valuable to encourage students to incorporate the skills they are learning in their language arts classes into their Spanish-class activities. Again, your communication with the language arts teachers may result in better transference of skills into the second-language classroom as students' confidence and competence in writing increase.

Suggestions for Teaching Culture

Each regular unit of *¡Hola!*, *¿Qué tal?*, and *¡Adelante!* contains two sections related to culture: *¿Sabes que…?* and *Así es….* Each *¿Sabes que…?* section presents three or four facts about Spanish-speaking countries. Each *Así es …* section presents a short paragraph on a selected topic. In addition, photographs, charts, and simulated real-life documents in the different units provide access to other aspects of everyday life in Spanish-speaking countries. By observing these photographs and realia and answering questions, students begin to formulate ideas about the diversity of Hispanic peoples.

These elements are simply an introduction. They should, by no means, be the sole means of integrating culture into the program. In the Unit Plans section of this *Annotated Teacher's Edition*, you will find suggestions and information that will help you incorporate cultural instruction into your daily lessons. On-page annotations also include cultural information about photos and realia.

In addition, the *Culture Resource Book* provides you with blackline masters of activities and information that you can incorporate into your teaching.

Cultures are not static. They change and evolve over time. Therefore, it is important to build the skills students will need to gather information, make observations, and formulate general and specific conclusions. It is also important to develop a nonjudgmental appreciation of the way of life of other people.

As students gain competence and confidence in communicating facts and opinions about their own world, they can develop an awareness of those same aspects of culture in the Spanish-speaking world. They can begin to recognize similarities and differences through observation. They can begin to experience how behavior is affected by culture through role-play activities, research projects, and interviews with native speakers.

In addition to the many photographs in the textbooks, it is recommended that you use maps, slides, and other visual aids to lay the foundation of basic skills and information. For example, students may need to learn first that geography and climate greatly affect how people live before they investigate a specific region of the Spanish-speaking world. Likewise, they may need to recognize first that in their own culture, life in a big city differs from life in a small town or rural area before they can appreciate the same differences in other cultures. The following suggestions will help you to add variety to the teaching of culture in the classroom as well as to build skills that will aid students in understanding other ways of life.

- Use maps and globes to help identify areas of the world where Spanish is spoken—including in the United States. Whenever possible, have students locate specific countries and areas being discussed or depicted and then determine the relationship of that area to the place where they live.

- Show slides, filmstrips, and videotapes. Visual aids that relate to the theme of a unit can begin to make cultural information more concrete and meaningful. For example, with the increased prevalence of Spanish-language television programs, students may be exposed to aspects of the culture that previously would have required them to visit the culture. Practical examples of greeting and leave-taking, food, homes, family life, popular music—all may be depicted in programs broadcast on the Spanish-language networks.

- Use Internet resources. A wealth of information is accessible on-line. In addition, you might have students begin e-mail pen pal exchanges.

- Invite native speakers to the class. As often as possible, it is recommended that you invite native speakers—neighbors, exchange students, business people—to interact with the students. Preparation for the visit may consist of presenting background information on the visitor, such as country and city of origin, having students research the country, preparing suitable questions for the visitor in advance, and so forth. Likewise, the visitor will need information about what the students are studying and questions they will ask.

  Activities following the visit can include writing thank-you notes, conducting discussions about what the students learned, and assigning further research.

- Create a cultural environment. If you have your own classroom, you may display artifacts, create culture corners, and provide a "lending library" of resources and references for information gathering. Through records, cassettes, and radio programs, you can expose students to the diversity of music in Spanish-speaking countries.

Suggestions for Correcting Errors

Maintaining a nonthreatening, positive classroom environment and nurturing students' confidence in their abilities to communicate in the second language are the first requirements for successfully correcting students' errors. For many teachers who have been schooled in traditional methods of teaching, this means altering their own behavior patterns before they can effectively encourage linguistic accuracy in their students.

At one point or another, most people who have acquired a second language have experienced the frustration of trying to communicate a message while a well-meaning second person interrupts at every third or fourth word with corrections of agreement, verb tense, or pronunciation. The level of frustration rises to such a point that the message is lost, the speaker's confidence is shaken, and the corrections offered with good intentions are forgotten. Even worse, fear and reluctance to communicate in the second language replace the initial enthusiasm and joy at communicating a message.

This is not to say that errors should not be corrected. Making mistakes is a natural, inevitable part of the learning process. If left entirely alone, mistakes may become deeply ingrained bad habits. If corrected in a positive, nurturing way, they can be eliminated without creating anxiety in the learner.

Knowing What and When to Correct

In general, researchers have shown that teachers who select the errors to be corrected at the proper time can be more effective than those who correct by the interruptive reflex method.

In student speech and writing, it is important to correct errors that interfere with overall communication. That is, if an error makes a message unintelligible, it should be corrected. If an error creates a barrier to listening and reading, it should be corrected. In the literature on second-language instruction, these errors are called global errors, in contrast to minor, local errors. If a global error is made frequently, it is important to correct that error first, while temporarily ignoring a smaller error or slip within the same message. Researchers have also shown that correction is effective at the time of practice, for example, while doing exercises that follow a pattern. Conversely, correction can have an adverse effect when given while students are earnestly communicating freely, for example, during paired interviews or conversations.

Knowing How to Correct

Guiding students to discover an error for themselves and to correct it on their own has generally proven more effective than supplying the correct answer or form for them. The following suggestions have been gleaned from the literature on techniques of error correction in the second-language classroom.

One approach to correcting through gentle guidance is to repeat what the student has said up to the point of the error. Often this will cue the student to recognize the mistake and then correct it alone.

S: Me duele las manos.

T: (*holding up two hands*) **Hay dos manos. Me ...**

S: Me duelen las manos.

Another possibility is to provide an on-the-spot multiple choice, thus allowing the student to choose the correct response (e.g., **¿Me duele las manos o me duelen las manos?**). If the student has had sufficient initial input and modeling, he or she will be able to recognize the correct response and choose it. You can also correct an error by supplying your own response to serve as a model (e.g., **A mí no me duelen las manos. Me duelen los pies. ¿Qué te duele a ti?**).

Students may make an error or fail to respond when they do not understand the question or do not fully understand what is expected of them. In these instances, you may rephrase or restate the question or provide additional models to clear up the confusion. A confusing word or expression can also be cleared up by either allowing the student to see it in writing or, if the phrase is familiar from oral work, to hear it spoken.

In summary, it is important to be sensitive to your students' affective as well as cognitive needs. Especially for early adolescents for whom peer approval is important, techniques that guide, nurture, and support yet correct their efforts without damaging their self-esteem are far more effective than those that are perceived as being humiliating. Sarcasm, impatience, and interruptive, reflex-action correction have no place in the *¡Viva el español!* classroom. The humiliation and anxiety experienced when students' every utterance is corrected improperly can be permanently harmful and not only reduce their willingness to speak but also destroy their enthusiasm for learning.

Your efforts in studying and applying the research on error correction in the second-language classroom will be rewarded in your students by their positive attitude and willingness to take communicative risks.

Suggestions for Structuring the Class Period

Spanish language instruction is far from standardized; the number of classes, length of class periods, and class size and composition are as varied as the schools in which they are offered. *¡Viva el español!* has been structured to provide flexibility and ease of adaptation to fit almost all needs of Spanish-as-a-second-language instruction.

Multisection Class Periods

A multisection class period allows the freedom to adapt activities to fit the structure of any situation. Each section of a class period serves to keep the routine familiar, yet interesting and stimulating, by virtue of the variety of activities.

◆ The Warm-up serves as a transition from the first-language environment into the target-language environment. It affords a brief period for students to "switch gears" and begin thinking and responding in Spanish.

◆ Review activities may act as reminders of material recently learned or of vocabulary and structures learned some time previously. These review activities may take the form of continuing games, "show and tell," brief role-play activities, pencil-and-paper puzzles, or even a rereading of a passage or conversation. Numerous suggestions for review activities are listed in the Unit Plans section of the *Annotated Teacher's Edition*.

◆ Presentation periods include the presentation and/or explanation of the core vocabulary, language structure, conversation, or culture concept corresponding to the appropriate section of the unit being studied.

◆ Activities allow students to use the target language in varied situations by completing exercises, interviewing classmates, preparing Big Books, etc.

◆ Closing activities briefly wrap up the class session.

The following skeletal daily lesson presents suggestions for allotting time for each section of a class period. It is expected that you will modify the times and activities to reflect your own classroom situation and instructional objectives.

Multisection Class Period

Time	Section	Activities
2-5 min.	Warm-up	Quick questions and answers **(¿Cómo estás? ¿Qué día es hoy? ¿Cuál es la fecha? ¿Qué tiempo hace?** etc.) Brief relay game, chain activity, song, etc.
5 min.	Review	Games Oral presentations; role-playing Audiocassette exercises TPR activities Paired or small-group activities
5-15 min.	Presentation	Learning activities corresponding to the unit being studied Introduction of vocabulary or language structures, etc.
5-15 min.	Activities	Textbook or workbook exercises Guided oral practice Games Paired, small-group, or large-group activities or projects Individual or small-group informal assessment Extension or enrichment activities/projects
3-5 min.	Closing	Riddles, rhymes, songs Summary of the day's lesson

Assessment in
¡Viva el Español!

Assessment and evaluation of progress in acquiring a second language play an important part in sustaining students' enthusiasm for language learning, and offer you vital feedback necessary for tailoring your teaching to the needs of individual learners. In second-language learning, because students are constantly being asked to produce responses or react to communicative stimuli, there are frequent opportunities for assessment. However, because of the nature of communication and language production, there are different strategies required for assessment and evaluation. The *¡Viva el español!* program offers you frequent, creative opportunities and ideas for carrying out these vital functions.

Types of Assessment

Assessment in second-language learning needs to operate at a number of different levels, because of the many layers of skills and proficiencies that are being acquired, and that thus need to be assessed and evaluated. The types of assessment fall into three major categories: proficiency, achievement, and prochievement. Furthermore, each of these categories can be assessed through both formal and informal means.

Proficiency Assessment

Since the goal of our language teaching is to develop communicative proficiency in students, we must find ways to assess that proficiency. Proficiency assessment seeks to determine what students can do with the language they've been acquiring, and to what extent they can transfer that language into real-life settings that require them to both receive and give information—the act of communication. The emphasis in proficiency assessment is on performance.

There is, however, a "slippery" quality to communication that can make assessment difficult at times. There is not always a "right" answer. For example, there may be countless ways in which a student could respond to a given question or situation, each of which is appropriate. Students may give you answers you don't expect, ones that may take you by surprise, but that still respond directly to the question or situation you've posed. Students may also give responses that are imperfect on a structural or fluency level, but that nevertheless communicate a message that is understandable and appropriate to the requirements of the setting. Proficiency must be looked at in a very global, holistic way. You must constantly ask yourself the question, "Did I understand the message the student was trying to convey?"—and you must remain open and flexible in assessing what your students produce.

You should be aware that proficiency assessment can be very time-consuming, because it requires interaction with individual students or groups of students. For this reason, you may want to spread your assessments out over the entire course of the lesson, working your way through the class. Don't worry that some students will have had more opportunity to prepare for the assessment because they've had additional days of instruction. Language proficiency is not delineated with clear milestones, but is instead an evolutionary, holistic process that does not change dramatically from one day to the next.

Achievement Assessment

Achievement assessment looks at what students know, rather than at what they can do. Unlike proficiency assessment, achievement testing generally has answers that are right or wrong, and is relatively objective. It requires students to demonstrate retention of previously learned content material. In the case of language learning, achievement assessment can tell you whether students have learned specific vocabulary items, for example, or whether they know accurate endings for a verb or an adjective. As such, it is much easier to set objectives and to evaluate progress in this area. Historically, this sort of assessment has been the mainstay of language testing. However, as our goals have changed, achievement testing has taken on less importance. It remains, however, an important part of the overall assessment of student progress.

Prochievement Assessment

Prochievement is a word that has been coined to describe a type of assessment that combines characteristics of both proficiency and achievement testing. It asks students to demonstrate what they know in a meaningful context. Where traditional achievement testing has asked students to respond to isolated items, prochievement testing ties the items together in some sort of situation. You are still asking students to tell you what they know, and there are still right and wrong answers, but you come much closer to simulating communicative use of language. Prochievement assessment may also allow students to respond within a *range* of correct answers—i.e., there might be two or three acceptable responses to an item, but still there is an objectively "right" way of answering. Many of the activities and exercises in the student book follow this model, and lend themselves to assessment opportunities.

Formal vs. Informal Assessment

Each of the categories listed above can be assessed either formally or informally. In the case of formal assessment, students generally should be made aware that they are being assessed, and also be given some opportunity to prepare. It is important to give formal assessments regularly, though not so frequently that they become burdensome to you or your students. Formal assessments tend to create a great deal of anxiety in many students, and while valuable, may in some cases actually hinder the learning process. You should try to help the students understand your goals in assessing them, and make efforts to lower the stress surrounding this sort of testing. Avoid comparing students directly. Create an atmosphere in which individual students see formal testing as something between you and them, designed to help them, rather than to rank them. Formal assessment should usually result in some sort of feedback to the learner concerning performance so that the assessment does not serve as an end in itself, but rather as a tool for aiding the learner in understanding and improving. Suggestions for scoring or otherwise quantifying performance on formal assessments are discussed later in this article.

Informal assessments can be entirely spontaneous, and may be carried out even without the students' awareness. This sort of assessment does not necessarily result in a score or quantifiable outcome, but will still provide much valuable information for both you and your students. Informal assessment should take place as frequently as practical. It may be as simple as taking note of individual, pair, or group oral performance on an activity as you walk around the room, or as you read over written activities, or look over drawings and posters that arise out of an activity. It might also be more intentional, coming at the end of a presentation or sequence of practice and taking the form of a special set of questions that you ask students to respond to or a brief task that you ask them to perform. Virtually any activity in the text will lend itself to informal assessment.

Assessment Strategies

There is virtually no limit to the strategies that can be used in evaluation of language proficiency and achievement. In fact, it could be argued that anytime students produce language, you have an occasion for assessment and evaluation. Each teacher will need to find his or her preferred strategies and techniques based on individual teaching goals and requirements. However, there are some general principles and strategies that will assist you in finding creative solutions for your assessment needs.

"Assessment Opportunity" Helps

Throughout the *Annotated Teacher's Editions* of **¡Viva el español!** you will find numerous suggestions labeled as "Assessment Opportunities." These appear in the Unit Plans section at the front of each book and in the on-page annotations for the student pages. As you read through them, you will find creative suggestions for using the material in the student book, or in some way going beyond it, to find out what your students are capable of, both in terms of proficiency and achievement. In many cases, we suggest ways to vary items from an exercise that students have just been working on. We also offer ideas for linking the practice to real-life events that your students can relate to. We might suggest a game that will use the vocabulary students are learning, or we might give you some questions to ask to elicit particular vocabulary items or structures. Here are just a few examples:

◆ Ask students to borrow something from a classmate. Have them display on their desks the borrowed item plus one that is their own. Circulate around the classroom, choosing one item of the two on a student's desk, and asking, **¿De quién es?**

◆ Call out the names of teachers in your school. Have students respond by stating the subject each one teaches.

◆ State the following situations in English and ask students to tell you what they would say, using an appropriate **tener** expression: 1. It's 99° outside and the air conditioner is broken. (**Tengo calor.**) etc.

◆ Have students write the answers to three items of their choosing from Ex. B. Let them exchange papers and correct one another's answers.

You should not look at the "Assessment Opportunities" as the only occasions for evaluation. Look at them as ideas, and glean from them strategies that you can apply in other settings.

One-on-One Assessment

Particularly with younger learners, it can be difficult to find time to isolate yourself with one student to perform one-on-one evaluation. It would be ideal to find ways to do this that would afford some measure of interaction with a single student while still allowing you to maintain control over the class as a whole. This will most often occur while the class is working on a task that requires some quiet time, such as working on a writing project. Call students over to a corner of the room with you one at a time, or stand next to their desks and talk quietly with them. A few times a year, you might arrange "special project" days to allow yourself the opportunity for formal assessment, planning to spend two to four minutes with each student, perhaps over the course of two days. Some teachers have also had success with calling students at home, or working with them at lunch or recess periods, or having them record responses on cassettes that the teacher then listens to outside of class.

In practice, much of your one-on-one evaluation will need to take place "on the fly," as you call on individual students to respond, or as you look over a student's written work. Be careful to give all students opportunities for responding to you individually. It is very easy for extremely verbal or extroverted students to dominate in a second-language class where the emphasis is on communication. Introverted students or those struggling with the language will need some special opportunities to interact with you without fear of embarrassment.

Group Assessment

Group assessment is most easily conducted by observing and monitoring activity while the group is performing a task. Be sure to circulate from group to group. As much as possible, you should avoid interfering in the process, allowing students to interact with one another and correct one another. Evaluate students on their participation in the overall process, as well as on their individual contributions. A second assessment opportunity then exists when the product of the task is presented to the class. The *Entre amigos* and *¡A divertirnos!* activities throughout the program provide excellent opportunities for assessing group performance.

Portfolio Assessment

A superb technique for evaluation over time is afforded by portfolio assessment. By having students create portfolios of written work and projects, you end up with a series of "snapshots" of progress that can demonstrate for you and for the student what has been achieved over time. Furthermore, you have a product that can be revised, expanded, and improved by the student as new language is acquired, allowing you to compare new production with the benchmark of the original. Portfolios are also useful for motivating and involving parents in the learning process as they review what their children have been doing.

Many of the *Entre amigos* and *¡A divertirnos!* activities call for students to produce written work, drawings, posters, greeting cards, etc., all of which can be used to create a portfolio. In many cases, the *Entre amigos* practice will even ask students to go back and add to work done for earlier activities, refining or supplementing. You will also find a number of suggestions for student-created Big Books that would lend themselves well to this sort of assessment.

Peer Assessment

When treated sensitively, peer assessment can be an extremely effective tool. Because so many of the activities in the *¡Viva el español!* program are designed for pair and group work, students quickly become used to working with partners, and become comfortable with being assessed by a peer. Among other ways, this can be accomplished by having partners look over one another's work and make editing changes or corrections, by having students prepare short quizzes for one another, or by having a student listen to another student and note down the information he or she hears, and then check it with the person who gave the information. You might ask students to call one another at home in the evening and share information in Spanish. The next day, they can compare what they heard with what the other student thinks was said, and report on the accuracy of the communication. You can also give students checklists of objectives and other criteria for evaluating an activity, and ask them to evaluate the work of their pair or group based on those criteria.

It is important that students understand clearly from the outset that no harshness or unkindness will be tolerated when assessing or correcting their classmates. You will need to create a climate of trust and a sense of classroom community that will minimize the sometimes critical nature of early adolescents.

Self-Assessment

Students benefit when they learn that evaluation is not entirely the teacher's responsibility, and when they learn the value of assessing their own work. Portfolios, mentioned above, are excellent vehicles for teaching the art of critical review of one's own efforts. When quizzes are given, you might provide answer keys on overhead transparencies and ask students to check their own work. You could also provide checklists of objectives before an activity begins and have students rate themselves on how they attain the objectives at the end of the practice. Use the list of objectives on the first page of each student unit as one such checklist. Just before the unit test, ask students to read over the objectives that were set out and ask themselves if they can do each of those things, now that they've gone through the unit. If they find there are things they don't know how to do, they should report this to you so you have an opportunity for reteaching. Self-assessment comes more easily to some students than to others, and will require some practice.

Evaluation and Scoring

While some assessment is entirely informal and requires no quantification, there is still a need for scoring or tracking your evaluations. Particularly with formal assessment, you probably have district or state requirements for reporting an evaluation. Even informal assessments can lose their value for you if you do not record them in some way. There are a number of means of scoring or otherwise recording evaluations. The Testing Program that supplements the series has its own scoring system. Below are some ideas for scoring the other assessments you carry out in class. No matter what system you use, however, we sometimes have a tendency to look at the scores as a means of ranking learners, of proving what they don't know. Evaluation is much more useful when we look at it as an indicator of what students *do* know.

Achievement Evaluations

Achievement and prochievement evaluations are the easiest to score. Because items are objectively right or wrong, you can readily assign point values and keep track of them in a grade book. If you wish to record results of informal prochievement or achievement assessments, you might consider making simple tick-marks beside students' names in your grade book or on index cards to indicate successful responses. These can be tallied weekly and assigned a value. If you are not opposed to the idea of tokens, you might keep a supply of paper money or plastic tokens at hand. Each time students respond correctly, hand them one of the tokens. At the end of the week, they can turn the tokens in, and you can record a score based on the number of tokens.

Proficiency Evaluations

Proficiency evaluation can be tricky, given the subjective nature of language and communication, the virtually infinite number of responses that can be given in many situations, and the fact that communication can occur even when a response is flawed. If there is not a right answer, how can we score performance? To effectively evaluate proficiency, we need to look at a larger set of criteria. One such set could look like this:

- Did the student complete the communicative task?
- Was the message that was conveyed appropriate?
- How creative was the response?
- Was the response linguistically accurate?
- Did the student find ways to express ideas in spite of language limits?
- Did the student perform at ability level?
- Was progress demonstrated?

These lists of criteria could vary according to your personal goals and preferences. Once a set of criteria is established, a rating scale can be created. Obviously, not every one of the criteria is as important to communication as the others. This then calls for a weighted scale which gives more points to those factors that most affect communication, or that combines factors while still giving the greatest weight to communication. A simple scale might look like this:

Score	Performance
5	Excellent communication, almost no errors
4	Communicated well, but with noticeable errors
3	Communicated fairly well, but with many noticeable errors
2	Response understandable, but grossly erroneous
1	Practically incomprehensible
0	No response

The *¡Viva el Español!* Testing Program

A formal, self-contained assessment program accompanies each of the three textbooks in the *¡Viva el español!* series. For each level the Testing Program includes the following components:

♦ Testing Program blackline master book containing a detailed description of the program, suggestions and instructions for testing, blackline masters of the tests, an answer key for all written and oral tests, a complete tape-script of the audio Test Cassette, and a Student Progress Chart.

♦ Test Cassette with listening-comprehension activities corresponding to the oral testing sections in the Testing Program.

The components have been designed bearing in mind that students react most favorably to materials that are appealing and applicable to real conversation and that you, as a teacher, need testing materials that are pedagogically sound and easy to prepare and score.

Evaluation Techniques

The evaluation techniques and design of the *¡Viva el español!* Testing Program are compatible with the Natural Approach and Total Physical Response, approaches that stress the use of interesting and relevant materials, comprehensible input, and intense observation and involvement from students. The design of the Testing Program will help you create a nonthreatening testing environment in your classroom—an environment that allows sufficient success to encourage low to average achievers, yet stimulate high achievers and students who are gifted in second-language learning.

Test Types and Objectives

The *¡Viva el español!* Testing Program features two types of tests:
(1) a Placement Test to be administered at the beginning of the year and
(2) Unit Tests.

Placement Test

At the beginning of the school year, your students will fall into one of the following categories:

1. Absolute beginners

2. Novices (as defined by the ACTFL Proficiency Guidelines)

3. Students with three years of Spanish, using the *¡Viva el español!* Learning Systems

4. Students with some prior knowledge of Spanish from academic or real-life experience.

The Placement Test is designed to measure the language proficiency of students in groups 2, 3, and 4, giving you an accurate evaluation of each individual's current level of competence in Spanish. Since the instructional materials in the textbooks have been designed to accommodate all of the student groups listed above, the Placement Test makes no pass/fail distinctions. The test results, however, will provide scores that will enable you to compare your students' abilities and determine your teaching strategies. The Placement Test consists of a series of short subtests for evaluating your students' language skills (listening, speaking, reading, and writing) and their mastery of the elements of language (pronunciation, grammatical structure, and vocabulary). (For your information, the descriptions of proficiency for speaking, listening, reading, and writing at the Novice and Intermediate levels can be found in the *Resource Section* of this *Annotated Teacher's Edition.*)

Unit Tests

Besides the Placement Test, there are 12–14 Unit Tests in each package, including 10–12 individual unit tests, 2–3 review tests, a mid-year test, and an end-of-year test. The Unit Tests fully cover the skills and elements taught in the textbook and accurately reflect the content of the program. While the main purpose of the Unit Tests is to help you evaluate your students' progress in mastering the textbook materials, the tests can also serve as effective review activities when you return them and discuss them with your classes. The key goal of the testing program is to teach communication in context—not as an intellectual exercise nor as a reward or punishment. In a sense, the tests become another instructional tool in helping your students develop and refine their skills.

Conducting the Tests

Conducting classroom tests can resemble a balancing act in which you strive to preserve a nonthreatening atmosphere while you maintain students' enthusiasm for learning Spanish. The following key features of the Testing Program will help you achieve this goal:

♦ The familiar format of the Achievement Tests will build your students' confidence because students will recognize item types and pictures from their textbooks.

- The open, uncluttered appearance of the test pages, with a limited number of test items on each, enhances readability. Your students will feel a sense of accomplishment as they complete the pages in relatively short periods of time.

- The fact that the tests are not speed tests lessens student stress. Students have no need to "beat the clock" to finish a particular section.

In keeping with the concept of promoting mastery for all students, tests are not excessively "hard," but they do contain items at various levels of difficulty so that all students will be challenged. Suggested time limits for the tests are generous (20–30 minutes) because the tests are essentially power tests, rather than speed tests. As power tests, they generally contain fewer, relatively challenging items and allow students sufficient time to complete the entire test —as opposed to speed tests, which usually feature a large number of relatively easy items but do not allow students time to finish. The technique of having students exchange test papers and score them immediately in class is recommended. By reviewing tests right after taking them, students receive immediate feedback on their errors and have a chance to master materials not yet learned. The *¡Viva el español!* textbook series tests are designed for easy correction, and they feature useful, authentic sentences suitable for oral exercises.

Scoring the Tests

The *¡Viva el español!* Testing Program permits you to analyze test scores accurately and to give your students sufficient feedback in the form of meaningful numerical grades and positive learning reinforcement. The scores are not designed to be punitive; rather, they serve as markers for past achievement and as points of reference for further improvement. All tests allow for a separate oral achievement subscore. The Placement Test answer key includes guidelines for interpreting student scores to determine level of proficiency.

A Student Progress Chart is provided in the Testing Program blackline master book. On this chart, you can record your students' test scores, your informal assessment comments, and notes on individuals' strengths, as well as specific language skills that need improvement.

Parent and Community Participation in

¡Viva el Español!

Your students' parents or guardians and other members of the community can play a vital role in motivating students to learn and use Spanish and in reinforcing the importance of learning a second language and understanding other cultures. In this section, you will find suggestions for inviting parents to participate in the program, for increasing community awareness of the program, and for utilizing community resources.

Positive Parent Support

Laying the groundwork for parental participation begins with communication. It is equally as important to instill enthusiasm for second-language learning in the parents and members of the community as it is to foster and maintain enthusiasm in the students. At the earliest opportunity during the school year, you may share your program's goals and objectives with the parents, either at the first meeting of your PTA/PTO or through an open letter to parents, inviting them to learn about the *¡Viva el español!* program.

Explain the goals and benefits of learning Spanish simply and clearly to establish realistic expectations. In addition, you should explain the methodologies used to achieve the goals of communication and proficiency in Spanish to help parents understand the different kinds of exercises, activities, and projects their children will be working on during the school year. It is likely that any experience the parents may have had with learning a second language involved the grammar-translation method, the audiolingual approach, or another traditional approach to second-language learning. Therefore, their idea of how to learn a language should be brought up to date. An explanation of the approaches used in *¡Viva el español!* may likewise ensure parental support of and participation in Spanish language and cultural experiences outside the classroom.

You may wish to make a formal presentation at a PTA/PTO meeting, beginning with an overview of the program and following up with a sample lesson, including TPR activities, games, and textbook exercises. You may conclude with concrete suggestions for what parents can do in the home and in conjunction with school activities. Underscoring the relationship of parent participation and student achievement may instill in parents an essential awareness of their importance in the second-language learning process. Attitudes toward other languages and cultures are learned in the home. Starting out with a clear understanding of the Spanish language program in your school and the *¡Viva el español!* textbook series can pave the way toward fostering positive attitudes in parents.

Parent-Generated Activities

Whether or not the parents know Spanish themselves, they can do many things at home and with the school to encourage their children's interest in learning Spanish and to generate support for your Spanish-as-a-second-language program. The following suggestions have been selected from Gladys Lipton's *Practical Handbook to Elementary Foreign Language Programs*.* Parents can:

◆ Help the child see foreign words in newspapers and magazines or on labels on different products

◆ Purchase books and records at the child's level

◆ Keep in touch with the child's teacher to learn how they can help

◆ Assist the teacher by going on trips related to the foreign language work

◆ Talk to the class about their experiences in the foreign culture

◆ Speak to the class in the foreign language

◆ Speak to the class about their work in the foreign culture and opportunities for careers with foreign language backgrounds

◆ Encourage but not force the child to speak the foreign language at home

◆ Make sure that they let the child know that they are happy about the child's progress

◆ Serve on an Advisory Board for the school

---

* Gladys C. Lipton, *Practical Handbook to Elementary Foreign Language Programs* (Lincolnwood, IL: National Textbook Company, 1988), pp. 33-34.

◆ Try to give the child opportunities for participating in some aspect of the foreign culture at museums, on trips, on television programs, etc.

Parent involvement in the program may extend throughout the school year in conjunction with events and activities that enrich the language learning experience. To take advantage of the special skills and unique talents of your students' parents, you may wish to have them complete a resource questionnaire, such as the one on the following page.

Resource Questionnaire

Name(s) _____

Address: _____

Phone: Day _____ Evening _____

I (we) are willing to help

in the following way(s):

Please check one or more.

_____ Field trip chaperone

Days available: M   TU   W   TH   F

_____ Classroom aide for special units

Day(s) and hour(s) available: _____

_____ Provide (or demonstrate how to prepare) food for a "Tasting"

Dish and country: _____

_____ Demonstrate a craft related to Hispanic cultures

Craft and country: _____

_____ Speak about a career in which Spanish is used

Career: _____

_____ Speak about a trip to a Spanish-speaking country

Country: _____

_____ Share a special area of knowledge related to Hispanic

cultures

Area: _____

_____ Share a special skill in promoting or organizing events

_____ Publicity

_____ Community resources

_____ Other: _____

_____ Other ideas or suggestions: _____

_____

Increasing Community Awareness and Involvement

Periodic events, both large and small, not only serve to enhance the language-learning experience but also provide the opportunity for community members to become aware of and participate in your Spanish-as-a-second-language program. Many other programs in the schools receive public support and acclaim because they are highly visible and frequently publicized. Just as music programs hold concerts, athletic programs hold games and meets, and science programs hold competitions and fairs, your Spanish-language program can hold events to which the public is invited and in which community members can become involved. Even without knowledge of the language and cultures, parents and members of the community can share a memorable language experience, whether by attending a single event such as an annual ethnic dinner or fair or by participating in a series of events such as a "Foreign Language Week" or periodic field trips.

A special event may involve parents and the community in any or all of the following tasks:

- Publicity
- Printing
- Decorations

- Food
- Cleanup
- Entertainment

People in the community, both professional and nonprofessional, are often willing to participate in different phases of an event just for the asking. By drawing on the resources in your community, you can plan and implement activities that foster community support; bond parents, students, and the public in a shared experience; and provide an old-fashioned sense of community spirit. The following list may help you expand your contacts with the community:

Community Service

- paramedic
- librarian
- police officer
- firefighter
- postal worker

Recreation

- athlete
- disc jockey
- pilot or copilot
- travel agent
- flight attendant

Health

- exercise instructor
- nurse or nurse's aide
- physician
- dietitian

Science

- chemist
- florist
- conservationist
- zookeeper

Labor

- construction worker
- custodian
- mechanic
- painter
- landscape service

Other

- baker
- banker
- musician
- photographer
- secretary

In each of these fields, you may find willing guest speakers and volunteers for committees, as well as people who use Spanish in their work. Also, each field may have native speakers of Spanish who would be willing to talk to your students about what they do, how they use Spanish on the job, or even about non-work-related topics, such as family life and schools in other countries.

Selecting Events

Depending on the ages and interests of your students, you may select special events for the school year that not only offer varied linguistic and cultural experiences but also involve the community and parents. It is important to select a variety of events that take place at different times of the year, as well as at different times of the day. In many one- and two-parent homes, the parents work and are unable to attend events that take place during the school day. Scheduling events at varied times can ensure the participation of individuals who otherwise would be willing but unable to attend.

The instructional units in the *¡Viva el español!* textbook series serve as excellent points of departure for selecting events. *¡Hola!* begins with the immediate world of the student at school and spirals outward to the family; *¿Qué tal?* begins with the home and spirals outward to the community; and *¡Adelante!* explores the world at large. Each textbook contains themes that lend themselves to speaking and cultural events, as well as to single and week-long events. The following suggestions have been tried and found successful in fostering community and parent participation.

Ethnic Dinner /
Food Fair

An ethnic dinner or food fair may not be a new event, but it is, nevertheless, a tried-and-true event. For one evening, the school cafeteria or gymnasium can be converted into sidewalk cafes or little **restaurantes** that offer dishes from around the Spanish-speaking world. Volunteers may bring typical dishes that are representative of the countries. The recipes may later be written, printed, and bound into a booklet to share with the community. This event may be held in conjunction with a holiday and may include music, dancing, and exhibits.

Foreign
Language Week

To build enthusiasm for and awareness of the value of foreign languages, many programs sponsor a "Foreign Language Week." Activities may range from simple to extravagant, depending on your resources. The following suggestions are not exhaustive, but they may serve as starting points in planning activities:

- Label familiar places and items in Spanish (e.g., door, drinking fountain, principal's office, gymnasium, bathrooms, etc.) throughout the school.

- Decorate the halls with travel posters and/or have students make special posters about speaking Spanish (e.g., **¡Me gusta hablar español!**), visiting other countries, or using polite expressions (e.g., **Mi casa es su casa.**).

- Offer entertainment by the students, such as songs and other music, folk dances, and skits.

- Coordinate lunch menus to go with the foreign language theme (e.g., tacos, Spanish rice, etc.) or have a potluck lunch for the Spanish classes.

- Invite guests to show slides or movies or to give demonstrations of crafts (e.g., paper flowers, piñatas, etc.).

- If money can be obtained from a special school or PTA/PTO fund, a Hispanic entertainer or group could be hired to perform for a school assembly.

- Invite parents, teachers, and other students to visit your Spanish classes during the week.

- Display books and magazines from the Spanish-speaking world, as well as the Big Books students have created themselves.

- Invite speakers from the embassies or consulates in your state to talk about their countries.

- Establish a day when everyone will wear something related to Hispanic cultures or to speaking a foreign language (e.g., hats, sashes, buttons, iron-on decorations, etc.).

- Give all announcements over the public address system in Spanish and English and have all school menus and announcements printed in both languages.

Carnival

Near Pan American Day, students can hold a carnival. Each of the Spanish-speaking countries can be represented by traditional costumes, flags, music, products, or whatever makes each country unique. Students can plan a parade or develop skits or displays. They may also, with the help of their parents, contact community resource people for information or invite them to attend. Each Spanish class may also plan and staff booths for games.

Field Trips

Field trips can provide valuable language and cultural experiences in the real world. They can also give students first-hand experience with cross-cultural communication outside the classroom. A well-planned field trip involves everyone from parents and school administrators to community resource people. The following ideas may help you plan unique, enlightening field trips for your students.

- Television station. If there is a Spanish-language station or a station that features a Spanish-language program in your community, students may benefit from touring the station and meeting the media professionals, from announcers to film editors. A film editor or sound engineer may also be able to explain how programs are dubbed in other languages.

- Restaurants. A trip to a Hispanic restaurant may serve as a source of career information as well as a practical chance to use the language and learn about the culture. In conjunction with a unit on foods, students may learn about different spices and ingredients in many dishes and possibly watch the chef prepare a special dish.

- Bank. Any large bank usually has a person dealing with international currency. Students may learn about exchange rates and actually see foreign currency. In addition, they may explore career opportunities in finance and banking.

- Hospital. Students may meet health-care workers and observe first-hand how knowledge of a second language is important in health-related careers. Doctors, nurses, hospital dietitians, admissions secretaries, and paramedics may explain to students the need for learning a second language and the importance of communicating accurately and clearly.

- University. A university can be a tremendous source of field-trip possibilities. Trips may range from a luncheon with Hispanic graduate students to attending a performance or rehearsal of a visiting dance troupe.

- Bakery or grocery store. A trip to a Hispanic bakery or grocery store may introduce students to the food-service career field and acquaint them with many products whose origins are in Spanish-speaking countries.

- Courthouse. Many courts are open to visits from classes. The courts and lawyers frequently employ interpreters to help with the proceedings when monolingual Spanish speakers are involved in a case. Students may meet interpreters and ask questions about how they learned Spanish, what their work is like, etc.

- Chain store or gift shop. Many specialized chain stores and gift shops import items from other countries. Students may enjoy meeting the store's buyer, learning about the origins of handcrafted items, and hearing first-hand how knowledge of Spanish and Hispanic cultures is part of the everyday job.

Field trips can also be scheduled in conjunction with special community events and visits. Museums hold special traveling exhibits; civic centers often feature performances from foreign dance and musical groups; and city government officials often receive visits from dignitaries and business people from foreign countries. Keeping abreast of the activities in your community can result in rewarding field-trip experiences.

Career Day   Parents and others in the community can be a great resource for career-day speakers. Guest speakers and exhibitors can be invited to describe their jobs, talk about advantages and disadvantages, and explain how knowledge of a foreign language is useful and important. A career day may be planned with other teachers in the school or with guidance or career counselors who have many contacts with community resource people and who also may assist in scheduling and coordinating the event.

Planning for Successful Public Awareness

Successful programs almost always have successful public relations. You cannot expect the community to appreciate and rally behind your Spanish-as-a-second-language program if no one is aware of it. Gladys Lipton has underscored the importance of a successful public relations program as follows:

"There are some people who think that you do not publicize until the program has been running successfully for several years. This author does not agree with that philosophy. If the program has been very carefully planned, with input from many, many people, then the publicity will invite additional input from, perhaps, untouched sources, and that can only be a positive affirmation for the program.

"There are others who feel that 'hype' for a program, to use the vernacular for developing public awareness, is not a professional activity, is unworthy of educational goals. This point of view is not valid in today's world of accountability and taxpayers' sense of economy. Obviously, programs that go unnoticed and unpublicized do not capture the attention of policymakers. The first and foremost premise is that the program has to be educationally sound and effective, in terms of what the students are accomplishing. But a sound and effective program need not go unnoticed and unpublicized. As a matter of fact, having students demonstrate their achievements in the foreign language will help the program. It will also communicate to the students that they are, indeed, making great strides in their study of the foreign language."**

** Gladys C. Lipton, *Practical Handbook to Elementary Foreign Language Programs*
(Lincolnwood, IL: National Textbook Company, 1988), pp. 33-34.

The time and effort expended in developing and implementing an ongoing public relations program can benefit the school, the program, and the students.

Beginning the Public Relations Effort

Beginning a program of public awareness need not be a solo effort; in fact, it is recommended that you enlist the help and cooperation of others. Your public relations committee may include the school principal, interested parents, and teachers in other schools and disciplines, such as the high school journalism teacher.

One of the first steps in organizing your public awareness program is to identify your public. The right hand does not always know what the left hand is doing; thus, your public should include your colleagues in the school, administrators, members of the school board, guidance counselors, as well as students who are not enrolled in your program. Then public awareness may extend to parents, business organizations, educational associations, faculty organizations of colleges and universities, city government officials and workers, and other local and state groups and organizations. People inside and outside the school community need to know about your program, its goals and benefits, and the accomplishments of your students.

Once you have established your committee and identified your public, you will be ready to undertake the following tasks in a successful public relations program, as described by Lipton:

♦ Designate someone as the contact person

♦ Establish personal contacts with the media

♦ Plan for publicity before, during, and after an event

♦ Be scrupulously accurate with names, dates, places, etc.

♦ Show appreciation when you get publicity

♦ Plan to take black-and-white glossy pictures that can be submitted after an event (be sure to get everyone's name). Show children in action!

♦ Write press releases tersely, one page if possible

♦ Try to get specific information on deadlines, and work around them

♦ Be sure to give credit where it is due

- Stick to the facts!

- Have everything and everyone ready when reporters and photographers come to the school

- Don't be disappointed if you're turned down. Perhaps reporters will be able to come next time [†]

Carrying Out the Public Awareness Program

Your public awareness program can encompass a range of activities and products, from a brochure about your program to a "media event." Work with your committee to identify specific activities during the school year and then brainstorm the possible ways to publicize them. In all your plans and suggestions, do not overlook the students themselves. Your students can design flyers and posters, distribute leaflets, and enlist the help and cooperation of their parents or older brothers and sisters.

In addition to publicity for scheduled events and activities, be aware of opportunities that arise from unexpected situations and sources. For example, one of your students may use Spanish to perform a public service, such as helping an injured person; students and their families may plan to take or may have taken a trip to an unusual destination; you or your students may receive an award; an exchange student may visit or enroll in your class as a peer tutor. Focusing on human-interest aspects of foreign language study can be a boon to the media, who are always looking for positive, upbeat stories to round out the daily news.

Also, be open to invitations to speak to organizations in your community, as well as invitations to hold workshops in other districts. Speaking engagements can be a source of publicity in your community and elsewhere in the state.

Send frequent, well-written press releases. Not every event will be considered newsworthy; nevertheless, press releases serve as reminders that your program is a dynamic one that is worthy of attention. Press releases should never be longer than one page and should address the following questions:

- What is happening? What has happened?

- Who is involved?

- When will (or did) it take place?

[†] Lipton, *op. cit.*, p. 163

- Where will (or did) it take place?
- How will (or did) it happen?
- Why will (or did) it take place?
- Who is the person to contact for further information?

Press releases should also be timely. That is, be aware of the deadlines for the media. In general, allow two to three weeks before an event to contact the education editor of your local newspaper. Reporters and photographers must have time to schedule their visit or attend the event. At least that much time should be allowed to have your event announced as part of the local television or radio station's public service announcements.

If and when the media respond to your press releases, you should always follow up with a thank-you letter or phone call. A simple act of courtesy can go far in establishing a solid contact person with the media. In fact, someday that person may call you to find out what is happening in your program.

UNIT PLANS

In this section, you will find ideas, suggestions, and points of information corresponding to each unit and lesson in *¡Adelante!*

Each unit teaching plan is divided into two major sections: *Unit Overview* and *Strategies*.

In the *Unit Overview* section, you will find the communication, vocabulary, language structure, cultural, and recycling objectives for each unit. In addition, you will find a complete listing of the program components that correspond to each unit, as well as a list of other materials you will need to do one or more of the exercises and activities, or that you might want to bring in for enrichment activities or to assist you in presentation.

In the *Strategies* section, you will find ideas and teaching suggestions for each part of the *Student Textbook* unit: the *Unit Opener*, the *¡Hablemos!* and *¿Cómo lo dices?* sections, the various *Entre amigos* activities, as well as the unit closing *¡A divertirnos!* activity. For a listing and description of the various types of teaching strategies, see p. T-21.

To coordinate the different components of the program with the units and lessons, see the Planning and Pacing Chart on page T-30.

UNIDAD DE REPASO
UNIT OVERVIEW

OBJECTIVES

Communicate

- Exchange greetings
- Talk about parts of the body and what hurts
- Comment on clothes
- Describe people and make comparisons
- Talk about a house and the things in it
- Talk about where things are
- Discuss eating habits and preferences
- Talk about leisure activities and household chores
- Talk about daily routines

Build Vocabulary

This **Unidad de repaso** reviews salient vocabulary from *¿Qué tal?* including:

- Body parts
- Articles of clothing and adjectives for them
- Adjectives to describe people
- Rooms of a home and typical things found there, such as furniture and appliances
- Foods, including breakfast, lunch, and dinner foods and fruit
- People who typically work in schools

Structure the Language

This **Unidad de repaso** reviews salient grammatical structures from *¿Qué tal?* including:

- Indirect object pronouns with verbs such as **doler** and **gustar**
- Possession with **de**
- Adjective/noun agreement
- Use of **ser** versus **estar**
- Comparisons with **más...que**
- The irregular verbs **traer** and **poner**
- Expressions of location
- Present tense forms of regular **-ar**, **-er**, and **-ir** verbs
- Present tense forms of various stem-changing verbs, such as **poder** and **despertar**
- Present tense forms of reflexive verbs

Understand Culture

The cultural focus of the **Unidad de repaso** is on the world through the eyes of youth in Spanish-speaking countries, including their view of school life.

Recycle

The above objectives will serve as a guide to most of the language recycled in this **Unidad de repaso**.

PROGRAM RESOURCES

- Workbook, pp. 1–16
- Lesson Tape **Unidad de repaso**
- Resource and Activity Book
    Numbers Masters 166-176
    Letters Masters 177-180
- Testing Program, **Unidad de repaso**
  Placement Test (optional)

MATERIALS TO GATHER

- Index cards and markers *(Entre amigos*, p. 8)

STRATEGIES

UNIT OPENER (pp. 2–3)

Tap Background Knowledge

You may already be familiar with the abilities of the students in your class. If, however, you have a number of new students, you may wish to administer the *Placement Test.* The *Placement Test* will help you determine not only the levels of the students, but also the amount of review and practice of vocabulary and structures learned in *¿Qué tal?* that will be necessary.

See the introduction to the Testing Program blackline master book for complete instructions and suggestions for preparing students and administering the test.

Presentation Suggestions

The first few class periods should be devoted to reviewing classroom commands and

vocabulary and to other "refresher" activities, such as those suggested on p. 2 of *¡Adelante!* Such activities should be conducted in an unstructured fashion, allowing students to re-explore their Spanish skills in group conversations around a theme. Prompt with questions within the theme or with comments about yourself as necessary. Flexibility and spontaneity are desirable. At this point it is better to follow the students' lead and change the topic, if it will keep them talking in Spanish, rather than forcing a particular topic in order to elicit particular words or structures.

Suggestions for other first-week activities that will help create a nonthreatening, fun atmosphere include choosing Spanish names, practicing numbers, role-playing greetings and farewells, singing Spanish songs, and playing games such as "Simón dice."

You may wish to review the following sections of this *Teacher's Edition*:

- Methodologies, pp. T-13–T-18
- General Strategies and Techniques, pp. T-32–T-48
- The *¡Viva el español!* Testing Program, pp. T-57–T-59

Culture: Photos and Realia

See on-page notes, pp. 2–3.

Toward Cultural Understanding

After reading *¿Sabes que..?*, you may wish to explain the following:

In addition to hugs, it is also common for Spanish-speaking friends and family members to kiss each other on the cheek when greeting and leave-taking.

Many of the North American children who live much of the year in Spanish-speaking countries have parents who are in the military, in the diplomatic corps, or who work for North American firms abroad.

PRACTIQUEMOS
EXERCISES A–B (pp. 4–5)

TPR

Before launching into the activities, reacquaint students with Spanish classroom commands using a series of TPR commands. Consult "Useful Commands for TPR Activities and Classroom Exercises" (page T-36) as a guide to classroom commands that you will be using most frequently throughout the year.

Here is a brief summary of TPR procedures:

- Give a command and act it out. (Explain that you will be giving yourself a command.)
- Give a command, act it out, and have the class respond with you.
- Give a command to the class without responding to it. Students respond on their own.
- Give the command to small groups or individuals.
- Have students volunteer to give the command to their classmates.
- Students give commands to one another in pairs or small groups.

For a complete description of the TPR approach, see *Methodologies* (pages T-15–T-16).

Supplement and practice the commands by playing games from the "Games and Activities" resource section in this *Teacher's Edition*.

Presentation Suggestions

From the TPR practice described above, you may wish to lead a game of "Simón dice" as a warm-up to the body-parts context of Exercises A and B.

EXERCISES C-E (pp. 6–7)

Presentation Suggestions

Do Exercises C and E as whole-class activities, taking answers from student volunteers. Have students do Exercise D as a pair-work activity. Conclude by having volunteer pairs model selected exercise items for the class.

Extension

Play a guessing game. Describe an article of clothing worn by one of the students. The class must guess what the article is and who is wearing it—for example, **Es la camiseta de Jorge.**

Have students bring in pictures of their parents or grandparents when they were younger and present the pictures to the class, describing the items of clothing worn.

Bring various items of clothing to class, including odd ones such as beanies and feather boas. Invite students to try on items and ask a classmate's opinion of how they look or fit.

Critical Thinking

Use the context of clothing as a springboard to a discussion about stereotypes. You might use the Mexican **sombrero** as an example of a common North American stereotype about people's dress in other countries. Explain that, although North Americans still commonly imagine Mexicans wearing the **sombreros**, the hats are actually only sold as tourist souvenirs or perhaps worn as part of a traditional costume.

Challenge students to "put the shoe on the other foot" and come up with clothing stereotypes that people from Latin America might have about North Americans.

ENTRE AMIGOS (p. 8)

Presentation Suggestions

Review the meanings of the ten adjectives by playing the game of "Concentración." See the "Games and Activities" section of this *Teacher's Edition*. Play the game as a whole-class activity, using opposites as the matching pairs.

Encourage your visual learners to illustrate the words by drawing simple pictures on each card.

Cooperative Learning

Divide the class into small groups. Give each group the name of a well-known person. The group has five minutes to think of as many descriptive things to say about that person as possible. Follow up by having the group share their descriptions with the class.

Language Across the Curriculum

Language Arts Ask each student to choose a character he or she has recently read about in literature. Have students play the game in *Entre amigos* by pretending they are that character. Instead of picking a card from the second pile, students should base their answers on what they know or imagine their characters to be like.

EXERCISES F–G (p. 9)

Presentation Suggestions

Combine students into pairs of varying proficiency to do the exercises. Have students recombine in different pairs so as to do each exercise twice.

The Multi-Level Class

After completing Exercise F, challenge more proficient students to come up with statements using **menos...que**. For example, **Tu hermana es menos alta que mi hermana.**

Assessment Opportunity

Consider the use of portfolios to assess students' efforts and achievements over a given period of time. Have students use the questions in Exercise G to write a paragraph about their home. Include this paragraph in each student's portfolio.

EXERCISES H–I (pp. 10–11)

Presentation Suggestions

Distribute Vocabulary Cards of living room and bedroom furnishings from the blackline masters in the *¿Qué tal? Resource and Activity Book*. Have students respond to TPR commands and questions about the cards.

Give students one minute to write the names of rooms of a house across the top of a piece of paper: **el dormitorio, la sala, la cocina, el garaje,** etc. For each room, give them one minute to write as many objects as they can think of that are found there. You may wish to do one or two rooms a day at the beginning of the period as a warm-up.

Assessment Opportunities

To check for comprehension of expressions of location, place various objects on your desk and ask individuals about their positions in relation to each other.

To check for accurate usage of forms of **traer**, ask the question **¿Traes tu libro a la clase?** of the first student who enters the classroom. He or she must answer and ask the next student the same question before being seated. Continue until all students are seated.

To check for accurate usage of forms of **poner**, ask individuals where they put things at home. Some questions should elicit **sí** answers and others **no** answers. For example, T: **¿Pones tus zapatos en tu ropero?** S: **Sí, pongo mis zapatos en mi ropero.** T: **¿Pones tus camisetas en el horno?** S: **¡Claro que no! Pongo mis camisetas en mi tocador.**

EXERCISES J-L (pp. 12–13)

Presentation Suggestions

Have students look at the pictures in Exercise J and describe what people do with the objects. Have students repeat after you the names of the appliances to practice pronunciation. Do Exercises K and L as pair activities.

Before completing Exercise L, drill the present tense form of regular **-ar, -er,** and **-ir** verbs. Working with one verb at a time, call out a subject pronoun and have students respond chorally with the appropriate verb form.

Compare complete examples of the three regular verb conjugations on the board. Point out that the **-er** and **-ir** conjugations are the same except for the **nosotros/nosotras** form.

Remind students that the verb **tener** is irregular: **tengo, tienes, tiene, tenemos, tenéis, tienen.**

Language Across the Curriculum

Health/Science Have students work in small groups to create a nutrition chart in Spanish. The first column should include the names of the fruits found in Exercise K; in the second column, the vitamin and/or mineral content of each fruit; and in the third column, the part(s) of the body for which these vitamins are good—for example, **la sandía—vitamina A—los ojos.**

EXERCISES M–N (pp. 14–15)

The Heritage Speaker

Invite heritage speakers to describe eating habits in their countries of origin. Which is the most important meal of the day? At what time do people generally eat lunch? dinner? Ask them to think of possible reasons why eating habits are different from, or similar to, those in the U.S.

ENTRE AMIGOS (p. 16)

Presentation Suggestions

Before having students work in pairs on the *Entre amigos* activity, practice as a class using **gustar** and indirect object pronouns with food items. Invent a situation in which you must elicit students' opinions on plans for a dinner. (For example, the students are your relatives who are coming to visit for the weekend.)

Here is a conversation sample:

T: **Les gustan las legumbres, ¿verdad?**

S: **No, no nos gustan las legumbres.**

T: **¿Les gusta el pavo?**

S: **Sí, nos gusta.**

Ask volunteers to write on the board the final menu you decide on serving, based on the class responses.

The Multi-Level Class

For pair work activities such as in *Entre amigos*, it is often preferable to pair early- or pre-production students with more proficient students or heritage speakers. Having a strong partner will encourage them to participate.

EXERCISE Ñ (p. 17)

Presentation Suggestion

Do Exercise Ñ as pair work, using pairs of mixed proficiency.

Extension

After completing Exercise Ñ in class, you may wish to reassign it for individual written practice.

Re-enter/Recycle

Recycle the forms of **almorzar**. Arrange students standing around the room. Place some alone and others in pairs or groups of three or more. Circulate and ask with whom different students are having lunch. Ask students about themselves as well as about other groupings in order to elicit all the verb forms. For example:

Teacher:	**Pablo, ¿con quién almuerzas**
Pablo (next to Paco):	**Almuerzo con Paco.**
Teacher:	**Susana, ¿con quién almuerza Pablo?**
Susana:	**Pablo almuerza con Paco.**
Teacher:	**Pablo y Paco, ¿con quién almuerzan ustedes?**
Pablo and Paco:	**Nosotros almorzamos con Iris.**

EXERCISES O-Q (pp. 18–19)

Presentation Suggestions

You may want to do Exercises O and Q as written work to be handed in. Do Exercise P as a pair activity.

For the Nonspecialist

The verbs in Exercise O are reflexive verbs. The reflexive pronouns **me, te, se, nos,** and **os** are placed before the conjugated verb or attached to the end of the infinitive: **Ella se levanta temprano porque los niños quieren irse.**

Notice that **se** is used for several pronoun subjects: **él, ella, usted, ellos, ellas, ustedes.**

Extension

After completing Exercise O, have students write complete schedules of their days, starting with the time they wake up, proceeding through the school day, and ending with the time they go to bed.

The Multi-Level Class

After completing Exercise P, challenge heritage speakers and more proficient students to create similar questions for the whole class to answer.

EXERCISE R (p. 20)

Presentation Suggestions

Do Exercise R as a pair activity. Have the students who play Claudia interview more than one partner.

Re-enter/Recycle

Review the stem-changing verbs **pensar, tener,** and **querer**. Give students five minutes to write one sentence about what they plan to do on the weekend; one about what they have to do on the weekend; and one about what they want to do on the weekend.

ENTRE AMIGOS (p. 21)

Presentation Suggestions

As a class, have students brainstorm words in Spanish to describe personality and physical appearance. Write them on the board.

Also discuss writing strategies. One common strategy is to begin a paragraph with a general sentence that focuses on one aspect of the person, such as physical size, then add sentences giving details about physical appearance, such as hair color and eye color.

UNIDAD 1
UNIT OVERVIEW

OBJECTIVES

Communicate

- Talk about popular games, sports, hobbies, and other pastimes
- Talk about when and how to do these activities and who does them
- Talk about plans to engage in pastimes

Build Vocabulary

- Use words relating to pastimes, such as **jugador/jugadora, equipo, deporte, atleta, deportista, artista, volibol**

Structure the Language

- Use singular and plural forms of **jugar** (**u** to **ue** stem-changing verb) + **a** + noun
- Use **tocar** to talk about playing an instrument
- Use singular and plural forms of **ser** to describe self and other people, places, and things

Understand Culture

The cultural focus of **Unidad 1** is on sports, hobbies, games, and pastimes, and the role they play in Spanish-speaking cultures.

Recycle

Unidad 1 offers opportunities to recycle the following language:

- Comparison with **el/la** plus **más**

- Interrogatives: **¿cómo? ¿quién? ¿cuál? ¿cuáles?**
- Verbs: **hacer, querer, gustar, haber**
- Adjectives: **grande, pequeño, alto, bajo, fuerte, bueno, simpático**, etc.

PROGRAM RESOURCES

- Workbook, pp. 17–24
- Overhead Transparencies 1–4
- Lesson Tape **Unidad 1**, Exercise Tape **Unidad 1**
- Resource and Activity Book

    ¡Hablemos! Masters 1–3
    Vocabulary Cards Masters 32–41
    Vocabulary Review Masters 136, 137
    ¡A conversar! Master 154
    Numbers Masters 166–176
    Letters Masters 177–180
    Tape Exercise and Pronunciation
    Pages 1–2

- Culture Resource Book, Masters 1, 2, 3
- Test Blackline Masters and Tape, **Unidad 1**

MATERIALS TO GATHER

- Crayons, colored pencils/markers, index cards, pictures of people doing popular pastimes, sports, games, hobbies
- Games, equipment, and instruments
- Pictures of well-known athletes, musicians, etc.
- Schedules in Spanish of sports, games, and musical events

TRATEGIES

UNIT OPENER (pp. 22–23)

Tap Background Knowledge

To get your students thinking about this unit's subject matter, ask them what their favorite sports, hobbies, or pastimes are. Are there any hobbies they'd like to take up? What sports or games do they not enjoy?

Presentation Suggestions

Introduce the content of the unit by tossing a tennis ball to a student. Ask the student **¿Quieres jugar el tenis?** Encourage students to answer according to the example. Continue with four more students using football, baseball, basketball, soccer, and volleyball. Vary this by having Student 1, who catches the ball, answer the question, toss it to Student 2. Student 1 asks the question and Student 2 answers. Continue until most of the students have asked and answered.

Toward Cultural Understanding

Note that football is called **fútbol americano** and soccer is called **fútbol**. Tell students that in most Spanish-speaking countries, **el fútbol** is much more popular than **el fútbol americano**.

¡HABLEMOS! (pp. 24–25)

Presentation Suggestions

As you ask students the questions for this activity, act out another sport to indicate what they are going to do instead. Ask a student **¿Quieres jugar al tenis?**, as you act out shooting a basketball. The student should say **No, no puedo, voy a jugar al baloncesto.** After you've modeled this with a few students, ask a question and have the student act out a sport and say that he or she is going to do that instead.

Toward Cultural Understanding

Ask a student to read *Así es…* aloud. Explain that in general, some of the same sports that are popular in English-speaking countries are also popular in the Spanish-speaking world. Tennis is widely played, and baseball is a very popular sport throughout the Caribbean, Mexico, and Central America. Professional baseball players born in such places as the Dominican Republic and Cuba have come to the United States to play in the Major Leagues.

PRACTIQUEMOS (pp. 26–27)

Presentation Suggestions

For Exercise A, model one or two of the sports yourself, saying whether or not you like them. Give students the option to say that they do not like a sport, and to ask a partner whether he or she likes it.

For Exercise B, model the example conversation with a proficient student and then have students practice in pairs. Circulate to give help.

Enrichment

In groups of four or five, allow three minutes for students to compare lists and decide which sport is the most/least popular. Assign a student from each group to report results. Which is the least/most popular sport in the class?

ENTRE AMIGOS (p. 27)

The Heritage Speaker

Ask heritage speakers if they can name a famous person from their country who plays the sport that they draw from the bag. You might ask them to say a little about that person to the class.

¡HABLEMOS! (pp. 28–29)

Presentation Suggestions

Invite a student to read aloud **¿Cómo pasas el tiempo?** Focus students' attention on the pictures of pastimes. Invite volunteers to say which pastime is fun (**divertido**), difficult (**difícil**), easy (**fácil**), interesting (**interesante**). For example, **El tenis es difícil.** Invite a student to read the **¿Quieres jugar...?** question aloud. Direct students to form the question by using different vocabulary items and pointing to the pictures. Encourage other students to answer.

Practice the second conversation in the same way. Conclude by reviewing both conversations, having students use vocabulary items from both pages.

PRACTIQUEMOS (pp. 30–31)

Presentation Suggestions

Invite students to repeat the conversation **¿Quieres jugar...?** after you or the Lesson Tape. Then ask a pair of students to repeat the model and demonstrate the first example for the class. Have students practice in pairs.

Language Across the Curriculum

Health Ask students to recall what they've learned in health class regarding the healthful benefits of different sports. Why do they think these activities are good or bad for you?

Assessment Opportunity

Direct students to write the answers to Exercise A on paper and hand them in to you. Check answers for correct activities.

Extension

Post enlarged *Resource and Activity Book* Vocabulary Cards across the chalkboard. Write a variety of names and pronouns under each (**Mari y Juan, yo, tú, usted, ustedes, las muchachas, Carolina, Señor González**). Direct students to write questions for each in their notebooks (**¿Quieren jugar al ajedrez Mari y Juan?**). Students exchange notebooks and write corresponding affirmative answers.

ENTRE AMIGOS (p. 32)

Presentation Suggestions

Have one or two volunteers ask you the question. Answer, then ask the question of that same student, modeling both the question and the answer.

Re-enter/Recycle

You might phrase the questions as **¿Qué deporte es tu favorito?** Remind students that **¿qué?** and **¿cuál?** are similar words that are used differently, depending on the structure of the question.

Extension

After most of the students have had an opportunity to practice asking and answering, have them write three short paragraphs that tell what they found out about the other students in the group. They may also wish to include information about themselves. **(Mari no tiene un deporte favorito, pero su juego favorito es las damás. A Mari le gusta tocar el violín porque hace música bonita. Es difícil. Practica todos los días por la tarde.)**

Encourage students to read their paragraphs aloud.

¿CÓMO LO DICES? (pp. 33–34)

Presentation Suggestions

Ask a student to read the instructions aloud. Model each example, asking students to repeat after you and point to corresponding pictures. Ask students what they notice about the way the different forms of **jugar** are spelled.

For the Nonspecialist

Note that **jugamos** is the only form of **jugar** that doesn't have a stem change. In the other forms, the **u** changes to **ue**.

Listening Comprehension

Read the following sentences aloud to students. Have them listen once without writing anything. Then, read them again, and have students write the activities they hear.

Voy a jugar al tenis.

Me gusta jugar al béisbol y me gusta jugar al ajedrez.

No me gusta jugar al baloncesto, pero a Juan le gusta mucho.

¿Te gusta coleccionar estampillas?

¡ÚSALO! (pp. 35–37)

Presentation Suggestions

Model the example with one student. Then divide the class into pairs for oral practice. Circulate to check for correct use of the contraction **al** and correct verb conjugation.

TPR

Call on a student by name: **¡Miguel! Muéstrame "jugar al tenis."** That student stands and pantomimes the sport in your sentence. Continue with other activities and students.

ENTRE AMIGOS (p. 38)

Presentation Suggestions

Ask students to spend a minute looking over the unit in their books before you begin writing words on the board. Ask them to think of sentences with words that their classmates are less likely to call out.

¿CÓMO LO DICES? (p. 39)

Presentation Suggestions

Ask students to examine and read aloud the sample sentences on p. 39. Try to get them to recall the different ways they have seen **ser** used. You may wish to write these sets of sentences on the chalkboard and have students form conclusions:

> To tell time: **Son las once menos diez.** OR **Es la una y media.**

> To state origin: **Somos de** (place). OR **¿Eres de** (place)**?**

> To express relationships: **Alfredo y yo somos amigos.** OR **Anita es mi hermana.**

> To express a characteristic or trait: **Mis amigas son atléticas.** OR **El Sr. González no es alto.**

> To state a job or profession: **Javier Gómez es enfermero.** OR **La señorita Ruiz es bibliotecaria.**

¡ÚSALO! (pp. 40–41)

Presentation Suggestions

For Exercises A and B, begin by first asking students whether the subject is singular or plural for each item. Write this information on the board. Then have students do the activity.

Cooperative Learning

Have groups of four or five make charts with the following positive adjectives across the top: **atlético/a, cómico/a, inteligente, generoso/a, bueno/a**. Then ask students to fill in each heading with names of fellow students who fit these descriptions. To close the activity, have one person report from each group.

Language Across the Curriculum

Language Arts Ask students if they've learned other descriptive words for themselves or others in another class. What words might they like to know for this unit?

ENTRE AMIGOS (p. 42)

Re-enter/Recycle

Before you begin this activity, review with students the concept of different adjective endings according to gender.

¡A DIVERTIRNOS! (p. 43)

Presentation Suggestions

You may wish to use several long pieces of butcher paper that can be extended around the room or hung in the library to make "comic strip murals" for this activity. You may want to recommend that students practice their thought balloon sentences in their notebooks before transferring them to butcher paper.

Assessment Opportunities

Have students draw pictures for some of the activities, instead of clipping magazine photos. Then have them label them with sentences saying what the people in the picture are doing. Include their drawings in their portfolio. Check captions for correct structures and vocabulary.

UNIDAD 2
UNIT OVERVIEW

OBJECTIVES

Communicate

- Talk about important jobs in the community
- Name places in the community
- Talk about knowing people
- Tell what people are doing right now

Build Vocabulary

- Name various occupations in the community, such as **médico/a**, **policía**, **dueño/a**, **empleado/a**
- Tell where the people who have these jobs work, such as **hospital**, **departamento de policía**, **compañía**, **almacén**

Structure the Language

- Use the irregular verb **conocer** + **a** to talk about knowing people
- Use **estar** + words ending in **-ndo** to tell what people are doing right now

Understand Culture

The cultural focus of **Unidad 2** is on the community in Spanish-speaking countries, including important occupations and places where people work.

Recycle

Unidad 2 offers the opportunity to recycle the following language:

- The verb **hacer**
- Present-tense regular **-ar** verbs
- Use of **ser** with occupations
- The irregular verb **querer**

PROGRAM RESOURCES

- Workbook, pp. 25–36
- Overhead Transparencies 5, 6
- Lesson Tape **Unidad 2**, Exercise Tape **Unidad 2**
- Resource and Activity Book
    ¡Hablemos! Masters 4–7
    Vocabulary Cards Masters 42–55
    Vocabulary Review Masters 138, 139
    ¡A conversar! Master 155
    Tape Exercise and Pronunciation Pages 3–5
- Culture Resource Book, Masters 4, 5
- Test Blackline Masters and Tape, **Unidad 2**

MATERIALS TO GATHER

- Index cards; crayons or markers (*Entre amigos*, p. 49)
- Pictures from newspapers or old magazines that should show people in school, playing games or sports, working, getting ready in the morning, going to bed at night (*¡A divertirnos!*, p. 63)
- Realia relating to Spanish-speaking communities; postcards and photographs that show people working

STRATEGIES

UNIT OPENER (pp. 44-45)

Tap Background Knowledge

Have students work in pairs to brainstorm about adjectives describing their city. Compile these adjectives into a large list on the board.

The Heritage Speaker

Invite students who have lived in or traveled to Spanish-speaking countries to describe communities there. Provide maps for pointing out countries, cities, and towns. Ask them to talk about police, firefighters, doctors, and people of other occupations in their communities. Ask them also about occupations that are common in their communities but that may be uncommon in the U.S.

¡HABLEMOS! (pp. 46–47)

For the Nonspecialist

The word for "fire" is **fuego**. A large fire is called an **incendio**.

Presentation Suggestions

With books open, have the whole class repeat each vocabulary word and conversation sentence twice after you. Then have individual students point to the pictures as they say the corresponding vocabulary words. Next, with books closed, have all students repeat the words and sentences again, in unison. Finally, have individual students point to the pictures in the book and name the people and their workplaces.

The Heritage Speaker

Ask heritage speakers to pretend to give a newscast about incidents involving doctors, police, or firefighters in their countries or communities. Have the rest of the class take notes on what they understand. Then ask students comprehension questions about the broadcasts.

Extension

When students seem comfortable with the vocabulary words and sentences, divide them into groups of four. Have them ask each other and answer questions such as **¿Quién trabaja en el hospital?**

TPR

Sketch a simple community map on the board. Label locations: **el hospital**, **el departamento de policía** and **la estación de bomberos**. Then, using the command **señala** (point to), have students identify these places on the map. First do this individually: **Señala el hospital**. Then use the plural **señalen** to have two or more students at a time point them out.

PRACTIQUEMOS (pp. 48–49)

Presentation Suggestions

Have a student read the instructions for Exercise A to the class. Then have all students write complete sentences in their notebooks telling what the people pictured do for a living: **La Srta. Gómez es bombera.** Then choose five other students; read one of the five sentences while the class checks answers. For Exercise B, have students practice orally in pairs, switching roles after the first two items.

The Multi-Level Class

During paired exercise, challenge more proficient students by showing how the questions in Exercise B can also be answered with plurals, even though the **¿Quién?** of the question is singular. Thus the answers become: **1. Los policías, 2. Los médicos, 3. Los bomberos, 4. Los policías.** Encourage the more proficient students to practice with the plural forms while the rest of the class practices with the singular forms.

Assessment Opportunity

Give each student a removable stick-on label containing the name of one of the six persons named in Exercise A **(Srta. Gómez, Sr. Peña, Sra. Castro, Sr. Solís, Srta. Agapito).** On the board or on a transparency, write or place similar labels naming the places where these people work **(hospital, estación de bomberos, departamento de policía).** Then have students affix the name labels next to the place labels they match.

Listening Comprehension

For listening practice ask these questions orally. They require only simple **Sí** or **No** answers:

1. **¿Es la Srta. Agapito policía?** (Sí.)
2. **¿Es el Sr. Solís bombero?** (Sí.)
3. **¿Es la Sra. Castro bombera?** (No.)
4. **¿Es el Sr. Peña médico?** (No.)
5. **¿Es la Srta. Gómez bombera?** (Sí.)
6. **¿Trabaja la Srta. Agapito en el hospital?** (No.)

7. **¿Trabaja la Srta. Gómez en el departamento de policía?** (No.)
8. **¿Trabaja la Sra. Castro en el hospital?** (Sí.)
9. **¿Trabaja el Sr. Peña en el departamento de policía?** (Sí.)
10. **¿Trabaja el Sr. Solís en la estación de bomberos?** (Sí.)

ENTRE AMIGOS (p. 49)

Presentation Suggestions

Divide the class into groups of four. Give each group eight blank index cards. Have a student from each group neatly write the eight occupation names listed, one per card. Then have another student read the game rules aloud in English. Do the **policía** pantomime as an example. Then invite students to guess and correct them if necessary, using the model. Have the class repeat the answer in unison. As students begin playing, instruct them to set cards aside as they are used.

Enrichment

Invite students to add to the lists of occupations in their textbook by helping them translate their own career choices. Here are examples:

agente de ventas	*salesperson*
astronauta	*astronaut*
cantante	*singer*
científico / científica	*scientist*
dentista	*dentist*
ingeniero / ingeniera	*engineer*
negociante	*businessperson*
periodista	*journalist*
veterinario / veterinaria	*veterinarian*

¡HABLEMOS! (pp. 50–51)

Presentation Suggestions

Bring in items representing each of the careers depicted; for example, an item of clothing with a price tag for **vendedor/vendedora**.

Hold these items up as you ask students the questions on pp. 50–51.

Listening Comprehension

For listening practice, point to the pictures and ask these five questions, which require only simple **Sí** or **No** answers:

1. **¿Trabajan los empleados en las oficinas? (Sí.)**
2. **¿Son los dueños los directores de la compañía? (Sí.)**
3. **¿Trabajan los obreros en el almacén? (No.)**
4. **¿Venden ropa los vendedores en el almacén? (Sí.)**
5. **¿Son los dueños empleados en las oficinas? (No.)**

Critical Thinking

After reading *Así es…*, teach students the word for a person who speaks two languages: **bilingüe**. Have students list ways in which learning Spanish can help them now and in the future.

PRACTIQUEMOS (pp. 52–53)

Presentation Suggestions

Have a student read the instructions for Exercise A aloud to the class. Then invite another student to point to the picture of Sr. Oteo and ask the class **¿Qué hace?** *(What does he do?)* Ask a volunteer to read the answer aloud. Then have other students ask classmates **¿Qué hace?**, pointing to the other pictures. For Exercises B and C, have students work individually, writing the answers in their notebooks. When they have completed both exercises, write all nine item numbers on the board. Send students to the board to write the answers to the items. Together with the class, correct the answers on the board and in their notebooks.

ENTRE AMIGOS (p. 54)

Presentation Suggestions

Use the eight cards with occupation names that students made for *Entre amigos*, p. 49, and make more, using both new vocabulary from this unit and any other occupations students learned through the **Extension** for the same activity. Have students stand in two rows facing each other. Show them how to play, using the example in their books. Then hand the ball to a student. Hold the cards face down for the student to select one.

¿CÓMO LO DICES? (p. 55)

Presentation Suggestions

First have the class look at the pictures in the student text and read the three conversations silently as you read them aloud. Then act out each conversation with students.

For the Nonspecialist

The personal **a** signals that the noun or pronoun following is the object of the verb.

¡ÚSALO! (pp. 56–57)

Presentation Suggestions

For Exercise A, have students work individually, writing the correct forms of **conocer** in their notebooks. When they finish, choose six students to write their answers on the board. Then have the whole class help you correct the answers on the board and in their notebooks.

For Exercise B, have students work in pairs. Read the English instructions aloud to them; then invite two students to model the initial conversation. Next, with books open, have the class repeat the initial conversation in unison. Allow students time to write the answers in their notebooks and to practice them orally. Circulate, observing and offering help as needed. Then have pairs of students act out their conversations for the class.

Perform Exercise C as a whole-class activity, taking answers from student volunteers.

ENTRE AMIGOS (p. 58)

Presentation Suggestions

Have the class form a circle. Hand each student one of the occupation cards from *Entre amigos*, p. 49. As students ask and answer questions with **conocer**, help them with vocabulary, structure, and pronunciation.

¿CÓMO LO DICES? (p. 59)

Presentation Suggestions

With books open to the pictures, have the class say each of the four presentation sentences twice. Then show students how the action phrases in boldface have two parts: the verb **estar** and a word ending in **-ndo (trabajando, comiendo, subiendo)**. Explain that in Spanish, as in English, these sentences emphasize action going on right now. Then have students describe what various people around the school are doing right now: **Los alumnos están comiendo en la cafetería.**

Extension

To show that these sentences are used for action happening right now, walk around, pick your book up from the floor or desk, and write on the board, saying as you do: **Estoy caminando/recogiendo el libro/escribiendo.**

¡ÚSALO! (pp. 60–61)

Presentation Suggestions

For Exercise A, have a student read the English instruction. Then invite two students to role-play the model conversation. Next have students write the four responses in their notebooks. Circulate as they compose their responses, helping them with vocabulary and structure.

For Exercise B, have students work in pairs. Have two students role-play the conversation, then instruct all students to write the questions and answers in their notebooks. Then have pairs of students read their conversations aloud so that all students can check their sentences for correctness.

For Exercise C, have students switch partners. Read the model aloud for them. Then write it on the board, showing how they must sometimes add and change words. Next have the students write the five responses in their notebooks. When they have finished, invite five students to each write a sentence on the board.

ENTRE AMIGOS (p. 62)

Presentation Suggestions

Invite two pairs of volunteers to demonstrate the activity, one pair making two or three complaints, the other responding with solutions in the present progressive. As the rest of the students do the activity, circulate to give help and make suggestions.

Assessment Opportunity

This exercise could be used as a performance assessment tool to assess students' abilities to contextualize the present progressive.

¡A DIVERTIRNOS! (p. 63)

Presentation Suggestions

Encourage students to bring in photos and other pictures of people engaged in different activities that the students are interested in. Use these pictures as well as the ones you have collected. Organize students into groups, giving each group several photos to prepare with captions. You may want to have students organize photos by themes: sports, school activities, hobbies, work, etc.

Language Across the Curriculum

Visual Arts Have students suggest ways to make the community collage more artistic (layout, colors, lettering, drawing a frame). Allow students extra time to decorate their collages. You may want to allow the class to vote on the most decorative one.

Unidad 3
Unit Overview

OBJECTIVES

Communicate

- Ask for things
- Give commands, instructions, and directions
- Talk about ways to get around a place

Build vocabulary

- Name places in a city, such as **la plaza, el mercado, el teatro**
- Use words which indicate direction

Structure the Language

- Use familiar singular commands
- Use singular and plural present-tense forms of the verb **pedir**
- Note patterns in stem-changing **-ir** verbs

Understand Culture

The cultural focus of **Unidad 3** is on cities in the Spanish-speaking world.

Recycle

Unidad 3 offers opportunities to recycle the following language:

- Names of food items
- The personal **a**
- Use of the verb **estar**
- Use of the verb **ir**
- TPR commands

- Vocabulary related to family members
- Vocabulary related to household chores

PROGRAM RESOURCES

- Workbook, pp. 37–46
- Overhead Transparencies 7–10
- Lesson Tape **Unidad 3**, Exercise Tape **Unidad 3**
- Resource and Activity Book

    ¡Hablemos! Masters 8–11
    Vocabulary Cards Masters 56–66
    Vocabulary Review Masters 140, 141
    ¡A conversar! Master 156
    Tape Exercise and Pronunciation Pages 6–7

- Culture Resource Book, Master 6
- Test Blackline Masters and Tape, **Unidad 3**

MATERIALS TO GATHER

- Postcards from cities in Spain and Latin America
- Maps of Spain and Latin America
- Slides of buildings that reflect the Arab influences in architecture
- Toy models of such items as buses, taxis, traffic lights, and other new vocabulary words in the unit
- Blank maps of Spain and Latin America
- Index cards (*Entre amigos*, p. 74)

STRATEGIES

UNIT OPENER (pp. 64-65)

Tap Background Knowledge

To set the stage for the unit, ask students to talk about visits they may have made to a new city. Find out what was most difficult for them to do in the new city. Ask how they got around. Find out if they have some favorite cities, and ask them what is most appealing about those places.

Presentation Suggestions

Refer to the artwork of traffic signs on these pages. Ask students to guess what the signs mean. See if students can supply the meaning of **la plaza, el mercado,** and **el parque.** Ask if they know of similar places in their city. Then ask students to brainstorm methods people in a large city use to get around.

Toward Cultural Understanding

The full name of the park in Madrid is **el Parque del Buen Retiro**. Parks are a very common feature of cities in Spain. Entire families go to the parks to engage in sports, meet friends, have a snack, and enjoy the parks' attractions. Sundays are especially popular for park visits.

The Heritage Speaker

Ask heritage speakers to talk about cities in Spain or Latin America in which they or a family member have traveled or lived. Invite them to tell how life in these cities is similar to or different from life in U.S. cities.

Language Across the Curriculum

Social Studies Using maps of Spain and Latin America, point out the locations of large cities in the Spanish-speaking world. Give students blank maps to fill in with the names of the cities you talk about.

Enrichment

Assign groups of students to research different cities in the Spanish-speaking world. (You may want to assign specific questions for the groups to investigate.) Work with the media specialist in your school to help the students carry out their research. Then have each group make an oral presentation about their city.

Language Across the Curriculum

Fine Arts Use slides to show historic Spanish buildings whose architectural style reflects Arab influences. You may also want to show buildings in Latin America to illustrate how these influences on style carried over into the Americas.

¡HABLEMOS! (pp. 66-67)

Presentation Suggestions

Have the class listen to and repeat the conversation and vocabulary after you or the Lesson Tape. Encourage students to point to the pictures as they say the words. Show toy models of the various vocabulary items, and have students keep their books open and orally name each item as you point to it. After some practice, repeat this procedure with the students' books closed.

Assessment Opportunity

To test comprehension and retention of new vocabulary, use toy models or individual pictures to portray the items. Ask students questions such as **¿Es el taxi? ¿Sí o no?**

Extension

Put students in groups of three. Once they have had several opportunities to listen to the vocabulary items named, have students practice saying the words as a group. After three to five minutes of group practice, ask individual students to name different objects for the other group members to point to.

Critical Thinking

After reading the *Así es...* information, have students think of ways in which a subway system might contribute to the life of a big city.

PRACTIQUEMOS (p. 68)

Presentation Suggestions

Invite a volunteer to read the English instructions. Have students work individually on the exercise, then pair off with a classmate to compare their answers. Encourage them to refer back to the *¡Hablemos!* pages when there are differences in their answers.

ENTRE AMIGOS (p. 69)

Presentation Suggestions

Organize the class into pairs. Before they start asking each other questions, have students sketch the streets where they live. Suggest that they show their sketches as they answer the questions.

¡HABLEMOS! (pp. 70-71)

Presentation Suggestions

Use pictures or slides of buildings or places in your area; have students say the vocabulary words as you show the different items.

TPR

Practice the commands **señala** and **señalen** as you have students point to the different pictures while you name the vocabulary items.

PRACTIQUEMOS (pp. 72–73)

Presentation Suggestions

Have students do Exercises A and B as whole-class activities.

ENTRE AMIGOS (p. 74)

Presentation Suggestions

Have a set of index cards ready. Model the procedure for the activity with a group of more proficient students. Then divide the class into small groups and circulate to give support. At the end of the activity, have groups compare point scores.

The Multi-Level Class

Organize the class into groups, dispersing the more proficient students throughout the groups. Suggest that groups make the cards together; the more proficient students can write the vocabulary on the cards while other students draw small pictures to indicate meanings. Save these collections of cards for future games.

¿CÓMO LO DICES? (pp. 75-76)

Presentation Suggestions

Use TPR commands with which students are familiar to introduce this structure. Tell students they are going to learn how to give commands themselves. Have them read pp. 75–76 and answer the questions. Then ask them to compare the commands in the section with TPR commands they have been using.

For the Nonspecialist

In Spanish, the singular informal command forms are the same as the third-person singular forms.

¡ÚSALO! (pp. 76–77)

Presentation Suggestions

For Exercise A, you may want to have students work in pairs. One student gives the command, then his or her partner pantomimes the response. Have students do Exercise B as a whole class.

Extension

Give students a list of familiar verbs with which to make up informal commands to give one another.

ENTRE AMIGOS (p. 78)

Presentation Suggestions

Say some sample commands to the class. Ask students to guess the people who might appropriately say them and the situations in which they might be used. Then point to individual students to act out the commands. After a few examples, organize the class into pairs to continue the exercise.

Assessment Opportunity

As students give and follow commands, listen for correct structure and vocabulary and for actions that match the commands given.

¿CÓMO LO DICES? (pp. 79-80)

Presentation Suggestions

Ask for volunteers to read the captions under the pictures. Talk about the changes in the verb forms. Write the conjugated forms of **pedir** and **vivir** on the board and have students compare the forms. Use these differences to introduce the stem-changing structure. After discussing the differences between the two verbs, have students look at the conjugated forms of **pedir, servir,** and **seguir** on page 80.

For the Nonspecialist

The Spanish verbs **pedir** and **preguntar** both mean "to ask"; however, **pedir** means "to ask for (something)," while **preguntar** means "to ask a question."

¡ÚSALO! (pp. 80–82)

Presentation Suggestions

For Exercises A and B, have students work individually, then compare their answers with those of a partner.

To prepare students for Exercise C, you may want to have them practice **seguir** by getting a group of volunteers to stand in line while you ask the question **¿Quién sigue a... ?** Use the names of the students in line. Then have a volunteer read the instructions for the exercise. Have students work in pairs to do the exercise. Encourage students to do the exercise twice, switching roles after one round.

Re-enter/Recycle

For Exercise C, remind students to use the personal **a** before each person's name.

¿CÓMO LO DICES? (pp. 82-83)

Presentation Suggestions

After students read the information about directions, set up paths in the classroom and have one or two students at a time move along the path turning left or right or going straight depending on directions you give: **a la izquierda, derecho, a la derecha.** Then invite other students to give directions.

¡ÚSALO! (pp. 83–84)

Presentation Suggestions

Have students work individually on Exercise A, then pair up students to check their answers. For Exercise B, be sure students look carefully at Gisela's map so they can trace her path as they give directions.

ENTRE AMIGOS (p. 84)

Presentation Suggestions

You may want to have students prepare itineraries before writing about their trips. These will serve as an outline for the narratives they will write, and also provide visual support as they share their stories.

¡A DIVERTIRNOS! (p. 85)

Presentation Suggestions

Provide students with a map of the neighborhood around the school. Have them write the directions according to the map. You may want to have partners check these directions against the map, suggesting improvements in the route as well as corrections in structure and vocabulary. Have students actually walk through the indicated routes after school if possible.

UNIDAD 4
UNIT OVERVIEW

OBJECTIVES

Communicate

- Identify and name modes of long-distance transportation
- Learn the names of countries and continents
- Identify and name countries in which Spanish is spoken
- Talk about your own nationality and those of Spanish-speaking people

Build Vocabulary

- Name modes and locations of travel such as **el avión**, **el barco**, **el aeropuerto**, **el puerto**
- Name the countries of North America: **Canadá**, **los Estados Unidos**, **México**
- Locate countries in South America, Central America, and Europe

Structure the Language

- Use capital letters for names of countries and lowercase letters for nationalities
- Identify and use the appropriate masculine and feminine endings for nationalities
- Use definite articles when appropriate before certain countries
- Use the word **en** to talk about how people travel

Understand Culture

The cultural focus of **Unidad 4** is on travel in Spanish-speaking countries.

Recycle

Unidad 4 offers opportunities to recycle the following language:

- Questions with **¿Dónde está...?**
- Verbs: **ser** vs. **estar**
- Prepositions: **de**, **en**, and **cerca de**

PROGRAM RESOURCES

- Workbook, pp. 51–58
- Overhead Transparencies 11–14
- Lesson Tape **Unidad 4,** Exercise Tape **Unidad 4**
- Resource and Activity Book

    ¡Hablemos! Masters 12–15
    Vocabulary Cards Masters 67–69
    Vocabulary Review Master 142
    ¡A conversar! Master 157
    Tape Exercise and Pronunciation Pages 8–10

- Culture Resource Book, Masters 7, 8
- Test Blackline Masters and Tape, **Unidad 4**

MATERIALS TO GATHER

- Picture postcards (*Entre amigos*, p. 91)
- Index cards (*Entre amigos*, pp. 95, 99)
- Butcher paper and paints or colored construction paper (*¡A divertirnos¡*, p. 103)

TRATEGIES

UNIT OPENER (pp. 86–87)

Tap Background Knowledge

To help introduce the theme of the unit, talk about travel: modes and reasons for traveling, places to travel, etc. Tell the class about any trips you've made to Spanish-speaking countries, and invite students to talk about any experiences they've had abroad.

Presentation Suggestions

Write the title of the unit on the board and have students repeat it after you. Use gestures and language students are already familiar with to elicit the meaning of the title.

Call on different students to read aloud the captions under the pictures. Clarify meanings if necessary.

Culture: Photos and Realia

Bring to class (and have students bring) pictures and artifacts from travel to other countries, especially to Spanish-speaking places. Join students in talking about the realia.

The Heritage Speaker

Have the heritage speakers explain what bus and train travel are like in their countries of origin. Encourage their classmates to ask questions.

Language Across the Curriculum

Geography Obtain an atlas to point out the different information available about Spanish-speaking countries: topography, climate, size, etc. You might have students research this

kind of information about a specific country, and then include a description in their portfolios.

Critical Thinking

After students have read and discussed the information in *¿Sabes que...?*, ask them if they or their parents also eat, watch television, or read on long bus or train rides.

Toward Cultural Understanding

Ask students to raise their hands and take a tally of who has ever traveled by plane. Explain that in most parts of Latin America, young people would be more likely to have traveled by train or bus, since these are the most common forms of long-distance transportation.

¡HABLEMOS! (pp. 88–89)

Re-enter/Recycle

Before students do the activity, warm up with a review of **¿dónde?** Say **¿Dónde está el puerto?** Then call on a student to hold up his or her book and point to the port. Repeat until several students have pointed out things in the picture.

Presentation Suggestions

To check for comprehension of the title, go around the room and ask students **¿Estás listo/lista para salir?** Play the Lesson Tape or act out the first conversation with a student. Next, have students repeat the vocabulary items after you as you point to the corresponding pictures on p. 88. Finally, have students substitute the different vocabulary items to make different versions of the conversation.

Then direct students' attention to the map of North America on p. 89. Practice the conversation in the same way as the conversation on p. 88.

PRACTIQUEMOS (p. 90)

Presentation Suggestions

Have students look at the pictures. Ask them to say the names of the different things. Then call on individual students to name the things as you point them out.

ENTRE AMIGOS (p. 91)

Presentation Suggestions

If necessary, go over the instructions with students. To provide a model, draw a large postcard on the board and work with the class to come up with a message. Next hand out index cards. Have students follow the instructions and write their postcards. On the reverse side of the cards, tell students to draw a picture of a scene to match the content of what they wrote. When students finish talking about their postcards, display them in the room.

The Heritage Speaker

Have heritage speakers bring to class postcards they have received from friends or relatives in Spanish-speaking countries. You might have them talk about what the person did or saw, according to the postcard.

Assessment Opportunity

Have students include their postcards in their portfolios. You might record or videotape students describing their postcards for an oral portfolio.

¡HABLEMOS! (pp. 92–93)

Presentation Suggestions

As students follow along in their books, read aloud the title and the sample conversation or play the Lesson Tape. Refer the students to the maps on pp. 92–93. Have them repeat the names of the areas and the countries after you. As you do so, tell them to point to each place on the corresponding maps. Conclude by having students create different versions of the conversation, substituting names of countries and regions from the *¡Hablemos!* pages.

Language Across the Curriculum

Language Arts You might have students look up in an encyclopedia what languages are spoken in other areas and countries on the maps. (**Haití**: Creole; **Belice**: English; **Francia**: French; **Portugal**: Portuguese; **El Norte de África**: Arabic, French)

PRACTIQUEMOS (p. 94)

Presentation Suggestions

Have students locate on a map or globe the countries mentioned in the exercise. Have them repeat the names of the countries after you.

Re-enter/Recycle

Challenge students who are asking the questions to use **¿cuál?** in place of **¿qué país?**: **¿Cuál está más cerca... ?** You might refer them to **Unidad 1** for a review of **¿cuál?**

ENTRE AMIGOS (p. 95)

Presentation Suggestions

To prepare the class for this activity, point out (or have students point out) the continents and regions on a world map or globe.

The Multi-Level Class

Have lower-level students write down and then pronounce the names of all the countries they learned in this unit. Challenge the higher-level students to refer to a map or globe and state the locations of the countries in the appropriate continent or region.

Assessment Opportunity

After students play the game, shuffle and hand out two cards to each student again. This time, have them read statements as they did for the game, and record these statements for their portfolios.

¿CÓMO LO DICES? (pp. 96–97)

Presentation Suggestions

Begin by writing the word **país** on the board. Above it, write **los Estados Unidos**. Next write the word **nacionalidad**. Above it, write **estadounidense**. Point to the different words as you have the class repeat after you. Have the students work in pairs to answer the questions. Then go over their answers with them.

Extension

Have students make statements about themselves, using the sample pairs of sentences as a model: **Soy de los Estados Unidos. Soy estadounidense.** You can also have students pretend they're from one of the other countries mentioned.

Toward Cultural Understanding

Note that although people born in the U.S. call themselves "Americans," Latin Americans also consider themselves Americans. For the sake of clarity, it is important to say in Spanish **Soy estadounidense** rather than **Soy norteamericano** or **Soy americano**.

¡ÚSALO! (pp. 98–99)

Presentation Suggestions

For Exercises A and B, refer students to the Appendix, p. 281, where they will find an extended list of countries and nationalities. Model the names and have students repeat after you.

Have students discuss what a **Fiesta Internacional** probably consists of. Ask students if they've ever attended a party with people from other countries and cultures. What was it like? What did they learn?

ENTRE AMIGOS (p. 99)

Presentation Suggestions

Work with the class to come up with a list of things and people. Write the words on the board for students to use during the activity.

Assessment Opportunity

After playing the game, give students blank sheets of paper and have them draw and label three of the items used in the game. For example, they might render **un zapato venezolano** as a shoe decorated with the colors of the Venezuelan flag.

¿CÓMO LO DICES? (p. 100)

Presentation Suggestions

Point out the preposition **en** in the captions. Review its various uses with students.

Have students repeat the sample sentences after you. Answer any questions students have about the use of **ir a** and its different forms.

Extension

Have students work in pairs or small groups to make up their own sentences with **ir a** and **en**. Then have the pairs or groups compare sentences with those of other pairs or groups. Next have them write original sentences showing other uses of **en**. You might have them share their sentences with the class.

Re-enter/Recycle

Review with students the rule they learned in **Unidad 1** about the contraction **al**. If they're going to a country that takes **el**, they should use **al: Voy al Perú**. However, if **el** is part of the official name of the country (**El Salvador**), the contraction is not used: **Voy a El Salvador.**

¡ÚSALO! (p. 101)

Presentation Suggestions

For Exercise A, have different students name the places in the pictures. As they do so, ask

them to write the Spanish words on the board. Have the class repeat the words after you.

Tell students to do Exercise B and then compare answers with a partner. Then call on students to write their answers on the board and to read them aloud as the whole class makes corrections.

Re-enter/Recycle

Review the differences between **ser** and **estar**. Point out to students the use of **ser** in the activities on p. 98 and have them contrast it with the use of **estar** in this activity (people's origins vs. location).

TPR

Draw a large map of South America on the board. Then have students label the different countries. Now introduce the command form of the verb **ir** (**Ve**). Call on different students and say, for example, **Ve al Perú en avión**. The student extends his or her arms to pretend to be flying in an airplane, goes to the board, and points to Peru on the map.

ENTRE AMIGOS (p. 102)

Cooperative Learning

Photocopy a portion of a U.S. map or have the group members work together to draw their own maps of their planned train trip. In each group, assign members to the following tasks: look up names of towns, rivers, and mountains in Spanish; trace the route of the trip onto the photocopy; and say what the places are in English.

Assessment Opportunity

You might record or videotape group presentations for student portfolios.

¡A DIVERTIRNOS! (p. 103)

Presentation Suggestions

Go over the instructions with students. Help them organize groups and assign group members different tasks. Visit the library with the class and ask the librarian to help the groups find the information they need.

When groups finish the project, have the members take turns reporting their information to the class. You may want to videotape the presentations for later review.

Language Across the Curriculum

Social Sciences Have students talk with their social sciences teacher about various aspects of their work on the project. Encourage them to show that teacher their work to get feedback.

UNIDAD 5
UNIT OVERVIEW

OBJECTIVES

Communicate
- Talk to and about travelers and people in the travel business
- Talk about planning a trip
- Discuss different places you can travel to
- Discuss what you and others are doing right now

Build Vocabulary
- Name travel destinations and planning activities
- Name some common geographical locations such as **la playa**, **el lago**, **el desierto**

Structure the Language
- Use the present tense of regular **-ar**, **-er**, and **-ir** verbs
- Use the irregular verbs **estar**, **ser**, **ir**
- Use the present tense of stem-changing verbs (**o** to **ue**, and **e** to **ie**)

Understand Culture
The cultural focus of **Unidad 5** is on identifying places and points of interest for visitors to Spanish-speaking countries.

Recycle
Unidad 5 offers opportunities to recycle the following language:
- Months and seasons

- Forms of transportation
- Places in the city
- Weather
- Adverbs of place
- Prepositions of location with **estar**
- Time expressions

PROGRAM RESOURCES
- Workbook, pp. 59–70
- Overhead Transparencies 15, 16
- Lesson Tape **Unidad 5**, Exercise Tape **Unidad 5**
- Resource and Activity Book
  - *¡Hablemos!* Masters 16, 17
  - Vocabulary Cards Masters 70–77
  - Vocabulary Review Master 143
  - *¡A conversar!* Master 158
  - Tape Exercise and Pronunciation Pages 11–13
- Culture Resource Book, Masters 9, 10–11
- Test Blackline Masters and Tape, **Unidad 5**

MATERIALS TO GATHER
- Posters, pictures, slides, videos, etc. of famous places or sites in Spanish-speaking countries (pp. 104–105)
- Maps of Spanish-speaking countries
- Travel brochures, tickets, guide books, etc.
- Crayons, markers or colored pencils
- Drawing paper

STRATEGIES

UNIT OPENER (pp. 104–105)

Presentation Suggestions

Have students brainstorm some of the places they have visited, and what they liked or disliked about them. Ask them what they did in order to travel to these places—what kinds of preparations did they have to make? Did they or their parents talk to a travel agent?

Have students look at the artwork and photographs and try to guess the meanings of the captions. If students have experienced travel in Spanish-speaking countries, have them tell the class about places they visited and experiences they had.

Tap Background Knowledge

To establish the context of the unit, ask students if they have traveled in—or seen videos or movies about—Spanish-speaking countries. Encourage students to bring in photographs taken in Spanish-speaking countries—either their own photographs or ones from magazines.

Culture: Photos and Realia

Decorate your classroom with posters and pictures of tourist sites in Spanish-speaking countries. Find brochures and pictures of Spanish-speaking countries from travel agencies or different countries' official travel bureaus. You may want to begin a picture file to collect such materials.

Language Across the Curriculum

Geography Tell students that many natural wonders are found in Spanish-speaking countries. Using maps or a globe, discuss key mountain ranges, lakes, deserts, rivers, beaches, and plains.

Toward Cultural Understanding

Unidad 5 gives students an overview of the variety of countries and cultures where Spanish is spoken.

Assign countries to pairs of students. Have them visit a travel agency or go to the library to find out the following information:

- How can you travel to that country?
- How much does a ticket cost?
- What documents do you need to visit that country?
- What are some of the famous natural features and sights there?
- What are some foods to try and souvenirs to buy?

Students should prepare their information to share with the class.

You may wish to contact one or more travel agencies in advance to secure permission and prepare them for students' visits.

¡HABLEMOS! (pp. 106–107)

Presentation Suggestions

Invite two volunteers to play the role of **viajeros** while you play the role of **agente de viaje**. Guide them through a brief scenario about making travel plans using vocabulary and concepts from the unit. Tell the other students to take notes. Some possible questions are: **¿Adónde quieren viajar Uds.? ¿Cuándo** piensan salir? ¿Cómo prefieren viajar? ¿En avión? ¿En barco? ¿Cómo van a pagar? ¿Con tarjeta de crédito? ¿Con dinero en efectivo? ¿Van a necesitar un hotel? ¿Un coche?

Then ask the class questions about the information discussed. Follow up by having students open their books and repeat the vocabulary after you or the Lesson Tape.

Now invite student volunteers to practice the two conversations, changing vocabulary items where appropriate. Have students try to create as many variations on the conversations as they can.

The Multi-Level Class

Call on more proficient students or heritage speakers to create and ask questions related to travel. Ask the rest of the class to answer them verbally or by pointing to flash cards or pictures while saying the Spanish word for that picture.

TPR

Collect pictures or objects that are representative of different geographical areas. Draw large maps of Spain, Mexico, South America, and Central America. Make cards with labels of areas such as **las montañas**, **el río**, or **la selva**. Using TPR, direct students to place these cards on appropriate spots on the map. Recycle vocabulary such us **cerca de** and **lejos de.**

This may be a good opportunity to introduce vocabulary such as **arriba** *(up, above)* and **abajo** *(down, below).*

You could also copy smaller maps, distribute them, and have students individually label places on their maps according to your directions. Use TPR commands such as **escriban, dibujen, pongan,** and **indiquen**.

PRACTIQUEMOS (p. 108)

Have students work as a whole class. Volunteer pairs should act out each conversation based on the picture and word cues.

Extension

Repeat Exercise A, substituting other verbs. For example, **¿Adónde viajas, Marta? ¿Dónde vas a pasar las vacaciones?**

ENTRE AMIGOS (p. 109)

Presentation Suggestions

Using the travel brochures, pictures in the textbook, and other realia, have students pair up as **agente de viaje** and **viajero/viajera**. Have them prepare a brief skit by writing down their questions and answers and presenting them to the class.

The Multi-Level Class

If students are reluctant to develop their own questions, you may wish to brainstorm some possible questions as a class activity and write them on the board.

You can also photocopy a list of possible questions, distribute it to students, and let them choose five questions to use.

¡HABLEMOS! (pp. 110–111)

Presentation Suggestions

If possible, bring to class newspaper ads for travel destinations or brochures from a travel agency. Ask questions such as **¿Cuánto cuesta un viaje a...?** Have student volunteers model the conversations, then have other students substitute vocabulary items to vary each one.

Cooperative Learning

Prepare a list of famous geographical sites in Spanish-speaking countries—for example, **Cordillera de los Andes**, **Río de la Plata**, **Desierto de Atacama**, **los Pirineos**. Have students work in small groups to find out where these places are located. They should list each country next to the correct feature. You can take students to the library or bring an atlas to class. Make a game of the activity by awarding prizes to the group that finds the greatest number of correct answers in a limited time.

Enrichment

Play "El ahorcado" (see "Games and Activities") to practice spelling skills. As students become familiar with the vocabulary, you may wish to play the game with sentences, instead of with individual words.

Toward Cultural Understanding

Draw students' attention to the map of Mexico. Explain that Mexico is a very popular vacation destination. Every year, tourists flock to the beach resorts at Cancún, Mazatlán, Acapulco, Ixtapa, Puerto Vallarta, and many other locations. There they enjoy Mexico's warm climate and thousands of miles of beaches.

Visitors also go to see the Aztec and Mayan ruins of Teotihuacán, Chichén Itzá, Uxmal, and Tulum. Mexico City, the capital, is built on the site of Tenochtitlan, an important religious center of the Aztec empire. Mexico City itself is a modern, vibrant city with many museums and cultural events that attract countless visitors each year.

PRACTIQUEMOS (pp. 112–113)

Presentation Suggestions

Have students do Exercise A in writing and correct their answers as a whole class. For Exercise B, copy the chart on the board and have student volunteers come to the front to role-play the different items.

Assessment Opportunity

To assess students' acquisition of vocabulary words, write words or phrases such as **la agente de viajes**, **el billete**, **la playa**, and **costar** on index cards. Have students take turns reading them aloud and using them in sentences.

Listening Comprehension

Read aloud the sentences in Exercise B to practice listening comprehension. Students must answer with their books closed, either orally or in writing. Remind students that they can use the chart on the board as an answer bank.

The Multi-Level Class

Challenge your more proficient students to come up with two more items for Exercise B. Have these students work in pairs to read their sentences aloud and come up with travel suggestions.

ENTRE AMIGOS (p. 114)

Presentation Suggestions

Have students record their answers in their notebooks. Circulate and offer help as needed. You may wish to have students prepare a chart in advance (or you may do so) to help them record their findings.

Language Across the Curriculum

Visual Arts Distribute large sheets of butcher paper. In small groups, have students create their own travel poster by drawing places or cutting out pictures and pasting them on the paper. Have them give their posters titles such as **¡Vamos a las montañas!**

¿CÓMO LO DICES? (p. 115)

Presentation Suggestions

Ask students to make up sentences using the verb forms found in the chart.

For the Nonspecialist

The **vosotros/vosotras** endings for the verbs in this section are **visitáis**, **corréis**, **recibís**. Today, **vosotros**, the second person plural, is used principally in Spain.

Enrichment

Use games and activities to review and reinforce these verbs, such as verb relays, "El maratón," or "Escoge tu número."

¡ÚSALO! (pp. 116–117)

Presentation Suggestions

Have students work on their own to do Exercise A in writing. For Exercise B, select pairs of students to act out each of the indicated conversations for the class.

Assessment Opportunity

Give students time to write answers in their notebooks, individually for Exercise A and with a partner for Exercise B. Collect these to informally assess if students are able to use regular present-tense verbs correctly or if they need additional review and practice.

ENTRE AMIGOS (p. 117)

Presentation Suggestions

Before students work with partners, have the whole class brainstorm a list of ten action verbs to describe daily activities. Write the list on the board.

Assessment Opportunity

Ask students to write a short paragraph— to be included in their written portfolios—describing what they and their families do every day.

¿CÓMO LO DICES? (p. 118)

Re-enter/Recycle

This unit provides many opportunities to re-enter and recycle material such as **ser** + **de**, **ir a** and **estar** + prepositions of location.

Use classroom objects and travel-related materials to ask questions with **estar**. For example: **¿Dónde está el folleto? ¿Está sobre el pupitre o debajo del pupitre? ¿Dónde está el Ecuador? ¿Está al norte o al sur del Perú?**

Use **ser** + **de** with countries by pointing to a map and asking **¿De dónde soy/es?**

Use vacation leisure activities and places with **ir a** with questions such as **¿Qué vas a hacer en la playa? ¿Adónde vas para montar a caballo?**

For the Nonspecialist

The **vosotros/vosotras** forms of **estar**, **ser**, and **ir** are: **estáis**, **sois**, **vais**.

¡ÚSALO! (pp. 119–121)

Presentation Suggestions

You may wish to have students recite the answers to Exercises A and B orally. Have students complete Exercise C in writing (to be collected as an informal assessment, if you wish).

Enrichment

Personalize each exercise by asking students to choose a family member or friend and write a sentence describing where the person is now (for Exercise A), what he or she looks like (for Exercise B), where he or she is going for vacation, and what he or she is going to do there (for Exercise C).

¿CÓMO LO DICES? (pp. 121–122)

Presentation Suggestions

Review the concept of stems by writing several infinitives on the board and erasing the infinitive endings. Have students state what the remaining letters are called.

Practice questions/answers with the verbs **poder**, **almorzar**, **probar**, **costar**, **querer**, **pensar**, **comenzar**, and **cerrar**. Have students create at least one question with each verb. Use as a daily warm-up or closing exercise. You can make it into a game by awarding points for correct answers and questions.

¡ÚSALO! (pp. 123–124)

Presentation Suggestions

Complete Exercise A orally with the class. As a follow-up, have students write out answers and turn them in. You may want to ask them to answer the questions truthfully and not according to the clocks on the page.

For Exercise B, have the class come up with three more questions before beginning pair work.

Assessment Opportunity

Call out a stem-changing verb in the infinitive and have one student use it in a question and another student use it in an answer. Repeat this exercise until you are able to assess students' usage of these verbs.

ENTRE AMIGOS (p. 124)

Presentation Suggestions

Have students compose a list of questions. Collect and correct them, then have students rewrite their questions with corrections. Suggest that students leave a line or two under each question for their partner's answers. Have them write the report on a separate sheet of paper.

The Heritage Speaker

Encourage heritage speakers to interview Spanish-speaking members of their communities about their vacation plans.

¡A DIVERTIRNOS! (p. 125)

Presentation Suggestions

If students are having difficulty coming up with a skit, you may wish to have the class as a whole brainstorm ideas.

Unidad 6
Unit Overview

OBJECTIVES

Communicative

- Talk about people, places, and activities related to air travel
- Learn some expressions commonly used in air travel
- Talk about what you and others do and say

Build Vocabulary

- Learn words relating to air travel, such as **aeropuerto**, **equipaje**, **piloto**, **vuelo**
- Talk about travel using expressions of time: **el vuelo número dos cincuenta y ocho (llega/sale) a las ocho y cuarto**

Structure the Language

- Use the present tense of **hacer**
- Use the present tense of **decir** and **decir que**
- Replace nouns with direct object pronouns

Understand Culture

The cultural focus of **Unidad 6** is on air travel in Spanish-speaking countries.

Recycle

Unidad 6 offers opportunities to recycle the following language:

- The use of **estar** plus the gerund

- The use of the personal **a** after a verb
- Adjective and noun agreement

PROGRAM RESOURCES

- Workbook, pp. 71–84
- Overhead Transparencies 17, 18
- Lesson Tape **Unidad 6**, Exercise Tape **Unidad 6**
- Resource and Activity Book

    ¡Hablemos! Masters 18, 19
    Vocabulary Cards Masters 78–85
    Vocabulary Review Master 144
    ¡A conversar! Master 159
    Tape Exercise and Pronunciation
    Pages 14–15

- Culture Resource Book, Masters 12, 13
- Test Blackline Masters and Tape, **Unidad 6**

MATERIALS TO GATHER

- Photos of airport scenes and personnel (pp. 126–127, *¡Hablemos!*, 128–129, 132–133)
- Old magazines for cutouts (pp. 126–127, *¡Hablemos!*, 128–129, 132–133)
- Old airline tickets (pp. 126–127, *¡Hablemos!*, 128–129, 132–133)
- Old suitcases or duffel bags (*¡Hablemos!*, pp. 128–129)
- Spanish-language television schedules from newspapers (*Así es...*, p. 133)

STRATEGIES

UNIT OPENER (pp. 126-127)

Tap Background Knowledge

Have students brainstorm what they know about traveling by plane, either firsthand or from TV or other sources.

Presentation Suggestions

Discuss the photographs, asking students to pick out as many details as they can. Invite them to say what the photographs and artwork remind them of, and to guess the meaning of the captions. Try to introduce unit vocabulary in the discussion. You may wish to use supplementary photos you have gathered to make previewing unit vocabulary more extensive. Ask one or more volunteers to read *¿Sabes que...?* on p. 127.

The Heritage Speaker

Students who have traveled to and from Spanish-speaking countries may have things to say about their air travel experiences. Encourage their input by asking questions such as: Where is the airport you left from? How did it differ from the one where you landed? Were important signs in more than one language?

Toward Cultural Understanding

Remind students that Latin America comprises all the territory in the Western Hemisphere south of the United States. You might want to mention that the region is called Latin America because its earliest European settlers spoke languages that derive from Latin: Spanish, Portuguese, and French.

¡HABLEMOS! (pp. 128–129)

Presentation Suggestions

Have students repeat the dialogue after you or the Lesson Tape. Then identify the pictured items and have their names repeated. Have students point to the pictures as they repeat the words. If materials are available, you might set up an "airport corner." Students can use old airline tickets, old suitcases, and similar items to practice the vocabulary.

Have students practice the conversations, substituting vocabulary items as appropriate.

For the Nonspecialist

Note that in this unit **el equipaje** is used to mean "luggage or suitcases." **La maleta** refers to a single suitcase.

Enrichment

Point out to students that **piloto** is the same in the masculine and the feminine form. Only the definite article identifies the gender. Have students brainstorm a list of professions and check to see which ones have masculine and feminine forms in English and Spanish. You might point out that these forms are language conventions that are changing in both languages as men and women perform fewer stereotypical roles.

Extension

Ask volunteers to role-play **el piloto/la piloto**, **la aeromoza/el aeromozo**, and **el pasajero/la pasajera.** Have students observing call out the appropriate title to identify each role.

Language Across the Curriculum

Science Explain that air is thinner at high altitudes, making it difficult for the body to get oxygen. Newcomers to high-altitude cities like La Paz may feel light-headed and even sick. People who live at high altitudes develop stronger hearts and lungs; their blood is unusually rich in red blood cells.

PRACTIQUEMOS (p. 130)

Presentation Suggestions

If students aren't familiar with the present indicative conjugation of **ver**, ask them to help you write the paradigm on the board before you continue with the exercise. Then have the class as a whole work on the items. Take answers from volunteers.

Listening Comprehension

Play a game of "Veo, Veo." Make photocopies of the appropriate Vocabulary Cards from the *Resource and Activity Book* to use as flash cards and distribute them to students. Then say: **Veo (a) el/la___.** The first student to stand up with the corresponding card gets to start another sentence with **veo.**

ENTRE AMIGOS (p. 131)

Presentation Suggestions

After reading the instructions, point out that there are many common things in an airport whose names students already know but which are not part of the unit vocabulary—for example, **oficinas, coches, gente, relojes,**

papeles. Tell students that any word will be acceptable as long as most students agree that such a person or thing could be found in an airport.

Language Across the Curriculum

Social Studies Discuss the fact that many modern airports are almost cities in themselves. Large international airports often contain banks, post offices, hotels, police stations, even bowling alleys, in addition to restaurants and other food service concessions.

Assessment Opportunity

Use this activity to assess students' progress in acquiring airport vocabulary and their use of definite articles **el** and **la.**

Extension

Obtain pictures of people in an airport, sitting in an airplane, etc. (Check airline advertisements for possible pictures.) Divide the class into pairs or small groups and ask them to describe the people and the scenes.

¡HABLEMOS! (pp. 132–133)

Presentation Suggestions

Read aloud the title and the dialogues and ask volunteers to repeat them after you. Play the Lesson Tape and point to new words as students hear them. Discuss the meaning of the expressions: **en realidad** *(actually),* **¡No me digas!** *(You don't say!)* and **a tiempo** *(on time).* Point out the relationship between **vuelo** and **volar—el vuelo** *(the flight)* is a noun; **volar** *(to fly)* is a verb.

For the Nonspecialist

Many common Spanish prefixes, because they come from Latin, have the same meaning in both Spanish and English. For example, the prefix **in-** (**incómodo**) usually means "not."

Enrichment

Obtain television schedules that use the 24-hour clock from Spanish-language newspapers. Have students practice reading the times on these schedules aloud.

PRACTIQUEMOS (pp. 134–136)

Presentation Suggestions

Make sure students understand that the schedule in Exercise A shows the time each flight is supposed to arrive. The time in the exercise is its actual arrival.

Have students look at the realia items in Exercise C. Ask them to find words that look similar to English words—for example, **agencia** (agency), **reservaciones** (reservations), **tarifa** (tariff), **destino** (destination). Write the cognates on the board or on a transparency.

Toward Cultural Understanding

In written examples of time in Spanish, a period is often used instead of a colon, as shown in the plane ticket on p. 136.

ENTRE AMIGOS (p. 137)

Presentation Suggestions

Read aloud the instructions in English, then call on volunteers to read the lists of places and people. Point out some of the comical names of the characters and ask students to look up or guess the meanings.

Cooperative Learning

Have groups of five or six "go all out" and turn their conversation into a dramatic production. Make sure that groups are prepared to make decisions cooperatively and that everyone has a definite role to play: set designer, script writer, actor, director, prompter.

¿CÓMO LO DICES? (p. 138)

Presentation Suggestions

Students should have little or no trouble with **hacer**, since its forms have been used as passive vocabulary throughout this course. The only new forms are **hago** and **hacemos**. Display the paradigm of **hacer** on the board and leave it in a visible place for the next two lessons.

For the Nonspecialist

Note that with the exception of the **yo** form, the endings for the present-indicative conjugation of **hacer** are the same as for regular **-er** verbs. Because the **yo** form ends in **-go**, **hacer** is sometimes called a **-go** verb. Other **-go** verbs that students know are **poner** and **traer.**

¡ÚSALO! (p. 139)

Presentation Suggestions

For Exercise A, explain to students that **hacer fila** means "to stand in line." Inform them that Exercise B presents a less idiomatic meaning of **hacer:** "to make." Have them do Exercise A as a whole class and Exercise B as a pair activity.

Re-enter/Recycle

Have students practice negation by restating the answers to Exercise A in the negative.

ENTRE AMIGOS (p. 140)

Presentation Suggestions

Have a volunteer read the English instructions aloud. Explain that students will probably not use **hacer** in their responses; they should give answers that are true for them. Groups of four or five are ideal. After all groups have finished, ask them to share results with the class.

¿CÓMO LO DICES? (pp. 141–142)

Presentation Suggestions

Introduce the use of **decir** by asking students a simple question and repeating what they say using **decir**. For example, ask: **Carla, ¿te gustan los plátanos?** If she says yes, turn to the class and say **Carla dice que le gustan los plátanos.** Then look at Carla and say **Carla, dices que te gustan los plátanos.** Try to use all the forms of **decir**. Review the illustrations and sentences on p. 141. Read the last two paragraphs and write the paradigm for **decir** on the board. Ask students what other verbs have the **-go** ending for **yo. (poner, hacer, traer)**

Listening Comprehension

Have each student write down a question in the form of **¿Te gusta...?** Divide the class in groups of three. Student 1 asks Student 2 a question and Student 2 responds. Student 3 must summarize with **Dice que le gusta...** or **Dice que no le gusta...**

¡ÚSALO! (pp. 142–143)

Presentation Suggestions

For Exercise A, have students review the meaning of **decir la verdad** (*to tell the truth*) and **decir una mentira** (*to tell a lie*). Have partners take turns making statements based on the pictures and responding with **verdad/mentira** statements.

For Exercise B, remind students that "He/she says yes" in Spanish is literally "He/she says that yes." **(Él/Ella dice que sí.)**

The Heritage Speaker

Heritage speakers may want to talk about **el Día de los Inocentes**, which is celebrated on December 28. Find out if their families played any practical jokes last **Día de los Inocentes.**

Extension

Play a form of "Gossip" by telling the first student in each row a sentence. The second student must ask what you said. The first student replies with your sentence. The third student asks what you said, and the chain continues to the end of the row. Vary the activity by handing students index cards with statements made by different people, such as **Piloto: Vamos a aterrizar.** Ask: **¿Qué dice el piloto?** The student should reply, **El piloto dice que vamos a aterrizar.**

¿CÓMO LO DICES? (pp. 144–145)

Presentation Suggestions

Read aloud the introduction and the examples on p. 144. As you read, make sure students understand what each pronoun refers to. Copy sentences on the board or on a transparency and have students draw arrows from each direct object pronoun to the noun it replaces.

Tap Background Knowledge

Invite students to define a pronoun—a word that takes the place of a noun. Then challenge them further by asking the difference between a subject and an object pronoun. Have students give examples in English of pronouns used as subjects *(I, you, he, she, we, they).* Ask what their Spanish equivalents are **(yo, tú /usted, él/ella, nosotros/nosotras, ellos/ellas).**

Tell students they already know how to use direct object pronouns in English *(me, you , him, her, us, them)* even if they don't know the term. Display parallel lists of English subject pronouns and direct object pronouns on the board for students' reference.

¡ÚSALO! (pp. 145–147)

Presentation Suggestions

For each exercise, call on volunteers to model the sample conversations. Point out that the conversations are always more fun when people really "get into" their roles. For Exercise A, encourage students to use the intonations and gestures of people who are hurried and nervous. For Exercise B, have students imagine different party situations such as a very sophisticated event where people behave very formally or a raucous party with loud music. For Exercise C, invite students to have fun with the part of the little brother.

Extension

Have pairs create a humorous skit between a parent and a child who is going out of town to visit a friend or relative. The problem is that the child has nothing ready for the trip. Have students make sure that the situation and its resolution are clear, then present their skits. Vote for the best skit and best actors.

ENTRE AMIGOS (p. 148)

Presentation Suggestions

Have a volunteer read the English instructions. Then call on two pairs of students to model the sample conversations. Once students understand how they're going to play the game, allow them time to generate a list of items and the places they would normally put them before breaking into groups.

Listening Comprehension

Say aloud sentences like **Conozco a Eduardo** or **Tengo los billetes en mi maleta.** Challenge students to repeat the sentence using direct object pronouns.

¡A DIVERTIRNOS! (p. 149)

Presentation Suggestions

Tongue-twisters are fun, but they can also be intimidating. Model them first with a heritage speaker or a very proficient student. Then give pairs five to ten minutes to practice. If you have a stopwatch, you can have a contest to see which pairs of students can read their **trabalenguas** the fastest.

Assessment Opportunity

Trabalenguas provide a good opportunity to evaluate students' level of pronunciation. Listen for mistakes in vowel sounds; help students review these sounds where necessary.

UNIDAD 7
UNIT OVERVIEW

OBJECTIVES

Communicate
- Name things commonly found in hotels
- Talk about things you and others do
- Talk about daily routines

Build Vocabulary
- Learn hotel vocabulary such as **la habitación, la llave, la toalla, el ascensor**
- Learn useful phrases and vocabulary, such as **el jabón, la bañera, la ducha, agua caliente**

Structure the Language
- Use the reflexive verb **dormirse** and other reflexive verbs
- Use the verbs **pedir, jugar** and other stem-changing verbs

Understand Culture
The cultural focus of **Unidad 7** is on hotels in Spanish-speaking countries.

Recycle
Unidad 7 offers opportunities to recycle the following language:
- Use of reflexive verbs to talk about daily activities
- Use of stem-changing verbs

PROGRAM RESOURCES
- Workbook, pp. 89–98
- Overhead Transparencies 19, 20
- Lesson Tape **Unidad 7**, Exercise Tape **Unidad 7**
- Resource and Activity Book

    ¡Hablemos! Masters 20, 21
    Vocabulary Cards Masters 86–94
    Vocabulary Review Masters 145, 146
    ¡A conversar! Master 160
    Tape Exercise and Pronunciation
    Pages 16–17

- Culture Resource Book, Masters 14,15
- Test Blackline Masters and Tape, **Unidad 7**

MATERIALS TO GATHER
- Keys, soap, towels; other vocabulary items
- Magazine pictures of hotel bedrooms and bathrooms
- Travel magazines, brochures, newspaper supplements
- Collection of hard and soft objects (*¡Hablemos!,* pp. 156–157)

STRATEGIES

UNIT OPENER (pp. 150–151)

Tap Background Knowledge

Begin the unit by talking about memorable trips students have had. Did they stay at a hotel? What impressed them the most? Tell students that learning about hotel etiquette and things they may need as tourists or travelers will make a visit to a Spanish-speaking country much more enjoyable.

Presentation Suggestions

Discuss the photos on p. 151. Have volunteers read the captions and try to figure out what the unfamiliar words mean from visual and context clues.

The Heritage Speaker

Invite heritage speakers to talk briefly, in Spanish, about an unusual travel experience they had. Remind them to use intonation and gestures to help their classmates follow.

¡HABLEMOS! (pp. 152–153)

Presentation Suggestions

Have the class repeat the conversation and vocabulary after you or the Lesson Tape. Have them point to the pictures as they read the words.

Extension

Set up a corner of the classroom as **la habitación**. Bring, or have students bring, as many vocabulary objects as possible to class. Use the corner for role-play, vocabulary practice, listening comprehension, etc. Introduce activities that will take place there with: **Vamos a la habitación.**

Critical Thinking

Remind students that an important part of learning a new language is to look for clues to meaning. These clues can come from context, words that look or sound similar to English words (cognates), or pictures. What clues can they find in words such as **habitación, turista, moderno,** and **antiguo?**

PRACTIQUEMOS (p. 154)

Presentation Suggestions

Have students work in pairs to complete Exercises A and B. Correct the exercises as a whole class.

Language Across the Curriculum

Language Arts Display the word **ascensor** on the chalkboard and ask students if they are reminded of any English word. Students may recognize the beginning of "ascend," a more elegant way of saying "to go up." Point out that learning a new language can improve the use of one's first language, too.

Listening Comprehension

Have students complete the sentences in Exercise A with their books closed while you read each sentence aloud. You might want to copy the words in the list for Exercise A on the board to help students choose their responses.

ENTRE AMIGOS (p. 155)

Presentation Suggestions

Bring to class, or have students bring, travel brochures and related material showing travel opportunities in Latin America and Spain. Compile a list of the 10 hottest spots, the places students really want to see—and be seen in! If students need more inspiration for a skit, tell them to think in terms of a mystery, or a comedy, a soap opera, or a heavy-handed drama.

¡HABLEMOS! (pp. 156–157)

Tap Background Knowledge

Have students list everything they would need or expect to find in a hotel room, including items of review vocabulary (for example, **una lámpara, una cama, un televisor**).

Presentation Suggestions

Read aloud the model conversations with a heritage student. Then go through the vocabulary illustrations asking comprehension questions, such as **¿Cómo está el agua, fría o caliente? ¿Qué hay en la cama?**

If possible, bring to class a pillow, a rock, and other objects to pass around to illustrate the words **blando** and **duro.**

Use pictures of things like ice **(el hielo)** and fire **(el fuego)** to illustrate the words **frío** and **caliente.**

The Multi-Level Class

Make copies of Vocabulary Cards from the *Resource and Activity Book*. Hand cards of adjectives to proficient students and cards of objects to those who are still building confidence. Ask students **¿Qué tenemos en la habitación?** and have them answer using the word on their Vocabulary Cards as a clue.

For the Nonspecialist

Point out the word **cajón** in the first dialogue and write it on the board. The ending **-ón** is an augmentative just as the **-ita** ending is a diminutive. **Cajón** is literally a big box; a **cucharón** is a very big spoon.

PRACTIQUEMOS (pp. 158–160)

Presentation Suggestions

Have students do Exercises A, B, and C as role-plays. Students should work in pairs, and change roles from one exercise to the next.

When students have completed their practice, invite volunteer pairs to perform selected items for the class.

Re-enter/Recycle

After Exercise A, review direct object pronouns and vocabulary by having students say where they would place an object after a hotel employee hands it to them: **¿Dónde pones la toalla? La pongo en el ropero o en el cuarto de baño.**

Language Across the Curriculum

Social Studies Are there any hotels in your area that have historical significance or are prominent features of your town or city? Have teams of students research a hotel in your community. Groups should present a report that covers things such as the age of the hotel, its history, how many rooms it has, what the busiest time of the year is, etc.

ENTRE AMIGOS (p. 161)

Presentation Suggestions

Have students work in a cooperative group to create a skit. Assign more proficient students to be writers; then assign other students as directors, prompters, actors, etc.

Enrichment

If a video camera is available, videotape the skits. Let groups use the tapes to analyze and improve their work. Students can perform their plays for parents or for other classes.

¿CÓMO LO DICES? (p. 162)

Presentation Suggestions

As a warm-up, review reflexive verbs by asking students questions such as **¿A qué hora te levantas? ¿Te peinas en las mañanas?** Read p. 162 aloud with students. Ask students to make sentences using each form of the verbs in the paradigm. Point out that **bañarse** is a regular -**ar** verb, **ponerse** is an irregular -**er** verb, and **dormirse** is a stem-changing verb.

Re-enter/Recycle

Remind students that **ponerse** belongs to a group called the -**go** verbs because the **yo** form ends in -**go**. What other verb do they remember from this group? **(decir, tener, salir, traer)**

For the Nonspecialist

Turning a nonreflexive verb into a reflexive one often gives a change in meaning to the verb. For example, **hacer** means "to make or do," but **hacerse** means "to become"; **ir** means "to go," but **irse** means "to leave"; **dormir** means "to sleep," but **dormirse** means "to fall asleep."

¡ÚSALO! (pp. 163–164)

Presentation Suggestions

For Exercise A, remind students to choose the most efficient logical order for the actions which are to come first or next. For Exercise B, these actions have to be made plural. For Exercise C, students have to make an appropriate choice of words based on the context of the sentences.

Critical Thinking

If students think Mario and his sisters have an unusual last name, they're right. Have them try to analyze the name, guess what it might mean, then consult a dictionary.

ENTRE AMIGOS (p. 165)

Presentation Suggestions

Have students think through the activities of a single day and list them in Spanish. Then have them decide on the activities they would do on their ideal day, the order in which they would do them, and finally the times for the activities. Have them share their activity statements with the other students in their group. Ask what similarities and differences in times and activities they notice. Have students attempt to work out any conflicts in the schedules for their "ideal" days.

Cooperative Learning

As anyone who has worked with a group can attest, getting consensus can be a frustrating experience. Make everyone responsible for their own schedule, but make it clear that the individual schedules shouldn't conflict with each other.

Assessment Opportunity

Use this activity to measure students' social as well as verbal skills. How do students compromise between their own needs and those of the group? Encourage students to use only Spanish once they have formed their groups.

¿CÓMO LO DICES? (p. 166)

Presentation Suggestions

Ask a student **¿Juegas al baloncesto?** As the student responds, write **juego** and **juegas** on the board. Ask another student **¿Qué juegan ustedes en la clase de gimnasia?** and write **juegan** and **jugamos** underneath.

Then ask students what verb you've been using. Write **jugar** on top of the column with a box around **jug-**. Explain that this part is called the stem. Have a volunteer draw similar boxes around the other verb forms on the board. What do they notice? Direct their attention to the **u** that changes to **ue** in all forms except the **nosotros** form.

Read the text and illustration dialogues on p. 166. You may want to have students do them as dictations.

¡ÚSALO! (pp. 167–168)

Presentation Suggestions

Do the exercises as a whole-class activity, calling on students to respond quickly to the various items.

Assessment Opportunity

Use the exercise practice as an assessment of students' oral skills and knowledge of new vocabulary and structures. Prompt responses also indicate a developing fluency and confidence with Spanish.

Extension

If any of your students have ever stayed in a hotel, ask them to make a list of items you can ask for in your hotel room using the verb **pedir**. To practice **jugar**, have them describe facilities in a hotel for playing games or exercising.

ENTRE AMIGOS (p. 168)

Presentation Suggestions

Encourage students to put themselves into the role of enthusiastic hotel guests. You may want to develop their ideas into a skit, with some students playing hotel guests, and others playing cooks, waiters, etc.

Re-enter/Recycle

As students enter the class, have them ask for their favorite food using the form: **Pido...** As each food is named, write it on the board, say it aloud, **Roberto pide...,** and let the student take a seat. If someone else has already asked for the food tell the student to ask for something else: **Carolina pide tacos. Pide otra cosa, por favor.**

The Heritage Speaker

Ask heritage speakers to create menus with typical dishes from their countries of origin to use in the role-play of a restaurant scene.

¡A DIVERTIRNOS! (p. 169)

Presentation Suggestions

Encourage students with musical skills to sing the song once for the class to follow. Then have all students sing the song. See if students can guess at the meaning of the lines.

Language Across the Curriculum

Music Ask students who play musical instruments to play the song while the rest of the class sings it.

Extension

Try doing the song as a round in three parts. One third of the class starts the song. After this group sings **Aserrín, aserrán,** the next third starts; after the first group sings **de San Juan,** the last third starts.

Critical Thinking

Invite students' opinions of this song. What do they think it is trying to say? How does it compare to English nursery rhymes?

Extension

Have students try the song using different forms of **pedir: Pido pan, no me dan,** etc.

For the Nonspecialist

In this song, **Aserrín, aserrán** literally means "Sawdust, they will saw." When spoken or sung, the words create a sawing noise—thus providing onomatopoeia. You might want to have students imitate the motion of a saw as they say this line. The translation of the song is as follows:

> Sawdust, they will saw,
>
> For the babies of San Juan.
>
> They ask for bread, they don't get any.
>
> They ask for cheese, they get a bone.
>
> Sawdust, they will saw,
>
> The little babies of San Juan.

UNIDAD 8
UNIT OVERVIEW

OBJECTIVES

Communicate

- Ask and answer questions related to banking
- Ask and answer questions related to restaurants
- Talk about giving
- Talk about what happens to you and to others

Build Vocabulary

- Name people and things found in a bank, such as **el cajero, la cajera, la ventanilla**
- Name people and things found in a restaurant, such as **el camarero, la camarera, el menú**

Structure the Language

- Refer to people and things by using indirect object pronouns
- Use the present tense and idiomatic expressions of **dar**

Understand Culture

The cultural focus of **Unidad 8** is on money and service transactions in Spanish-speaking countries.

Recycle

Unidad 8 offers opportunities to recycle the following language:

- Direct object pronouns
- Numbers from 1 to 1,000
- Use of **ser** with professions
- Foods
- Table setting items
- People in the school and community

PROGRAM RESOURCES

- Workbook, pp. 99–108
- Overhead Transparencies 21, 22
- Lesson Tape **Unidad 8**, Exercise Tape **Unidad 8**
- Resource and Activity Book

    ¡Hablemos! Masters 22, 23
    Vocabulary Cards Masters 95–101
    Vocabulary Review Master 147
    ¡A conversar! Master 161
    Tape Exercise and Pronunciation Pages 18–20

- Culture Resource Book, Masters 16, 17
- Test Blackline Masters and Tape, **Unidad 8**

MATERIALS TO GATHER

- Realia related to banks, including samples of foreign currency (*¡Hablemos!*, pp. 172–173; *Entre amigos,* p. 175)

- Realia related to restaurants and eating, including plastic foods or pictures of foods (*¡Hablemos!*, pp. 176–177; *Entre amigos,* p. 179)
- Foreign exchange tables from the newspaper (pp. 170–171; *Entre amigos,* p. 175)
- Play money (*¡Hablemos!*, pp. 172–173; *Entre amigos,* p. 175)
- Name tags and items to create bank and restaurant scenes (*¿Cómo lo dices?*, pp. 180–181, 184–185)
- Large index cards (*¡Úsalo!*, pp. 186-187)

TRATEGIES

UNIT OPENER (pp. 170–171)

Tap Background Knowledge

To establish the context of the unit, talk about the students' experiences with banks and restaurants. Call on one or two volunteers to share their experiences with the class. Invite students to bring in any foreign currencies they may have. Invite students to bring in any menus they may have, especially from foreign restaurants. In Spanish, ask questions about money and foods which recycle previous material. For example: **¿Cuántos centavos hay en esta moneda? ¿Cuántos dólares hay en este billete? ¿A qué banco van tus padres? ¿Cuál es tu restaurante favorito? ¿Qué te gusta comer en ese restaurante?**

Presentation Suggestions

Have students look at the photographs and try to identify which objectives listed on p. 170 correspond to which photographs. Ask students to guess the meaning of the photograph captions and individual words in the captions.

The Heritage Speaker

Invite heritage speakers to talk about the currency in their countries. Have them bring in any samples they might have. Help the class determine the value of the money in dollars by looking at the foreign exchange rate found in most newspapers. Have the heritage students discuss any banking experiences they may have had in their native countries or in the United States. You may also wish to discuss their favorite foods and restaurants in their native countries and in the United States.

Language Across the Curriculum

Math Tell students that each country has its own currency. The value of a currency can change from day to day. Using a foreign exchange table from a newspaper, show students how to change the Spanish **peseta**, for example, to dollars. Also show them how to change from dollars to **pesetas**. Have students bring their calculators to class. Students should round off the exchange-rate figures and make charts showing the number of **pesos**, etc., it takes to make one U.S. dollar, five dollars, and ten dollars.

¡HABLEMOS ! (pp. 172–173)

Presentation Suggestions

Point to **abierta** and **cerrada** in the illustration; ask students if they can guess the meaning of these words. Follow up by asking questions about places in your community. For example, **¿Están los bancos abiertos o cerrados a las diez de la noche?**

Have a pair of proficient students practice the conversations. Then have other students model the conversations, substituting different vocabulary items as appropriate.

Critical Thinking

After reading *Así es...*, ask students why they think every country has its own currency. Alternatively have students brainstorm the good points and bad points of all countries having the same currencies.

PRACTIQUEMOS (p. 174)

Presentation Suggestions

Have students work in pairs to quiz each other on the Spanish words for each of the pictures in the exercise. When they are sure of the vocabulary, have them say each item as a complete sentence.

Extension

After students have completed the exercise, you may wish to use the sentences for dictation practice.

ENTRE AMIGOS (p. 175)

Presentation Suggestions

Review the currency chart. Practice some of the mathematical calculations of currency values as explained previously. If possible, show actual samples of the currency. Have students bring in an up-to-date foreign exchange table from the local Sunday paper to use in their conversations. Use play money or actual currency as students role-play the currency transactions.

Language Across the Curriculum

Social Studies Have students choose a Spanish-speaking country and research the people that appear on different denominations of its money and report to the class. If possible, have students obtain examples of different currencies to show during their reports.

¡HABLEMOS! (pp. 176–177)

Presentation Suggestions

Have student volunteers role-play the first conversation. Ask students if they can substitute another new vocabulary item for any of the words in the conversation **(el camarero** for **la camarera).**

Continue with the second conversation. Encourage students to build short conversations of their own using the given conversations and vocabulary items—for example:

S1: **¿Vas a pedir el menú?**

S2: **¡Claro que sí!**

Re-enter/Recycle

You may wish to review vocabulary for food and table settings. Students may make or bring in play money, plastic or toy food items, or other realia with which to practice.

The Heritage Speaker

Invite heritage speakers to tell about restaurants in their countries. What are their favorite restaurants there? here? How often do families go to restaurants? Are fast-food chains popular in their countries?

Cooperative Learning

Have students prepare skits based on one of the following communication situations:

- Customer/server: The customer finishes lunch and discovers that he or she has no money to pay the bill—not even any coins for the tip.

- Bank teller/customer: The customer does not receive the correct amount of money from the teller (cashing a check or changing dollars for other currency).
- Two friends: One friend has just received $100.00 from a relative. The other friend helps him or her decide on how to use the money.

PRACTIQUEMOS (pp. 178–179)

Presentation Suggestions

Point out that Exercise A tells a story: each sentence is a moment in the speaker's day. Have students practice the individual sentences. They should then try reading the exercise as a monologue, with appropriate stress and intonation.

Have students do Exercise B as a pair activity: each partner gives an opinion about the item and its price.

The Multi-Level Class

Challenge your more confident students to complete Exercise A without looking at the unit's vocabulary. For the rest of the class, provide an answer bank from which they can choose their responses.

Enrichment

Have students guess the meaning of **preferir** from its similarity to the English verb. Point out that **preferir** is a stem-changing verb like **querer**.

For the Nonspecialist

Unlike the English "a thousand," **mil** does not require an article: **Un viaje por mil quinientos dólares.**

ENTRE AMIGOS (p. 179)

Presentation Suggestions

Allow sufficient time for students to plan the skit in class, collect their props, and write and rehearse the dialogue. Be ready to help students with ideas and language before the skits are presented.

¿CÓMO LO DICES? (pp. 180–181)

Presentation Suggestions

Point out that indirect object pronouns answer the questions "to whom" or "for whom" after the verb. Direct object pronouns answer the questions "whom" or "what" after the verb.

Use questions with **gustar** and **doler** to begin practice with the indirect object pronouns—for example: **¿A quién le gusta jugar al fútbol americano? ¿Te duele la cabeza antes de un examen?**

For the Nonspecialist

In Spanish, indirect object pronouns are always placed in front the verb, even in negative sentences: **No le pedimos la cuenta.**

¡ÚSALO! (pp. 182–183)

Presentation Suggestions

For Exercise A, be sure students understand that one friend is asking the other about the people who help him or do favors for him. Have partners take turns playing the part of Santiago. For Exercises B and C, students can work individually and correct their sentences with partners or in groups.

Extension

Have students work in pairs to expand upon Exercise A by creating some of their own questions and answers.

Cooperative Learning

After students individually complete Exercise C, have them get in small groups of three or four. Group members should check each other's answers and reach group decisions about which pronouns are correct.

ENTRE AMIGOS (p. 183)

Presentation Suggestions

Review the questions orally in class. Have students suggest additional questions or topics to include. Provide students with a checklist to help them correct their classmates' paragraphs. The checklist may include the following questions:

Is the paragraph clear?

Are there spelling or punctuation mistakes?

Are verb forms correct? Are indirect object pronouns correct?

Assessment Opportunity

Include the paragraphs and checklists in the students' written portfolios.

¿CÓMO LO DICES? (pp. 184–185)

Presentation Suggestions

Use realia items from this unit's vocabulary. Have some students wear name tags of people mentioned in the unit: **el cajero, la camarera,** etc. Students can then act out situations illustrating different forms of the verb **dar**—for

example: **Le doy las monedas al cajero.** Then ask the class **¿A quién le doy las monedas?** Call on someone to answer the questions.

TPR

Use TPR commands to practice forms of **dar**. For example, **Luis, dame un lápiz. Alumnos, ¿qué hace Luis?** Include idiomatic expressions: **Rita, dale la mano a Luis.**

Extension

Have students identify the indirect object pronouns in the example sentences on p. 184 and say to whom each pronoun refers.

¡ÚSALO! (pp. 186–187)

Presentation Suggestions

Have students work on Exercises A and B in pairs and put their answers in writing. Adapt Exercise C as a whole-class activity as follows:

Write each element of the answers— indirect object pronouns, verbs, and object nouns—on large cards. Organize students into groups of three and hand each group a set of cards. Play the role of Partner A, asking the questions. Group members must arrange cards in the correct order to form the answers.

Assessment Opportunity

Use these exercises to assess students' use of the verb **dar** as well as their speaking and reading abilities.

ENTRE AMIGOS (p. 188)

Presentation Suggestions

Prepare slips of paper in advance. Make sure everyone understands the rules. Allow five minutes for students to check their books and notes for occupations and how to spell them. To give students some extra preparation time, read aloud the names of the occupations as you place the slips of paper in the bag.

¡A DIVERTIRNOS! (p. 189)

Presentation Suggestions

Field trips require advance preparation with the restaurant, your school, parents, and students. Get a per-person price from the restaurant with tax and tip included. Collect all money in advance. Get a menu to practice ordering and incorporate it into class activities. Have students prepare five or ten questions in advance that they can use to make lunch conversation. Have all money counted and ready in advance so you can all enjoy the field trip. Review a few phrases like **¡Buen provecho! ¿Dónde están los servicios? Me falta el tenedor.**

Unidad 9
Unit Overview

OBJECTIVES

Communicate

- Name places in the community
- Talk about where people and places are
- Talk about how people are feeling
- Discuss meeting someone at a particular place

Build Vocabulary

- Learn names of more places in the city, such as **el museo, la iglesia, el teatro**
- Describe how people feel, using adjectives such as **contento/a, enojado/a, nervioso/a**

Structure the Language

- Use adverbial phrases such as **a la derecha** and **delante de** to describe the location of objects or places
- Talk about people and things using direct and indirect object pronouns
- Use **estar** to describe how people are feeling

Understand Culture

The cultural focus of **Unidad 9** is on urban life in the Spanish-speaking world.

Recycle

Unidad 9 offers opportunities to recycle the following language:

- The different uses of **estar**
- The present progressive
- Direct and indirect object pronouns

PROGRAM RESOURCES

- Workbook, pp. 109–118
- Overhead Transparencies 23, 24
- Lesson Tape **Unidad 9**, Exercise Tape **Unidad 9**
- Resource and Activity Book

  ¡Hablemos! Masters 24, 25
  Vocabulary Cards Masters 102–109
  Vocabulary Review Master 148
  ¡A conversar! Master 162
  Tape Exercise and Pronunciation
  Pages 21–22

- Culture Resource Book, Masters 18, 19
- Test Blackline Masters and Tape, **Unidad 9**

MATERIALS TO GATHER

- Art supplies, butcher paper, or poster board (*Entre amigos*, p. 195)
- Markers, crayons, drawing paper (*Entre amigos*, p. 200)
- Beach balls or foam rubber balls (*¿Cómo lo dices?*, p. 208; *Entre amigos*, p. 210)

STRATEGIES

UNIT OPENER (pp. 190–191)

Tap Background Knowledge

Begin the unit by having students name the cities in Latin America or Spain that they have heard of. Ask students what they know about those cities and in what ways those cities might be different from cities in the United States.

Toward Cultural Understanding

Many Latin American and Spanish cities have public squares, or **plazas**, where people congregate and relax with friends. **Plazas** sometimes have a market to which residents of the surrounding neighborhood can walk to shop for groceries or household goods. Shoppers go to the market often, even daily, buying only as much as they can comfortably carry each time. While at the market, they often meet their neighbors and friends who are also doing their daily shopping.

Enrichment

After reading the last *¿Sabes que...?* note, have students research some U.S. cities whose names derive from Native American cultures.

Assessment Opportunity

The photographs may be used for informal assessment. Ask questions—for example: **¿Qué hace el alcalde? ¿Dónde están los automóviles? ¿Qué hacen? ¿Cómo es la iglesia?**

¡HABLEMOS! (pp. 192–193)

Presentation Suggestions

Have the class repeat the conversation and vocabulary after you or the Lesson Tape. Then invite pairs to try to read the conversation as naturally as possible.

Toward Cultural Understanding

The Moors, the Arabic-speaking people who ruled Spain, were from North Africa. During the seven centuries of Moorish rule, many Arabic words became part of the Spanish language. Students can often recognize Spanish words that come from Arabic because many of those words begin with **al**. Have students point out the word in the conversation that is of Arabic origin. **(alcaldía)**

For the Nonspecialist

The mayor **(el alcalde** or **la alcaldesa)** may work in **la alcaldía** or in **el ayuntamiento**.

PRACTIQUEMOS (p. 194)

Presentation Suggestions

Read the English instructions and invite a volunteer to help you model the sample conversation.

Re-enter/Recycle

You may wish to write on the board or on a transparency a list of prepositions students have learned in previous units.

Extension

Have students work in pairs to write and practice their own short dialogues in which they make plans to meet each other at a particular place in the city. Have pairs present their dialogues to the class. To assess listening comprehension, ask the class where and when each pair of students is meeting.

Extension

Expand this activity by having students use other prepositions when answering their partner's questions.

ENTRE AMIGOS (p. 195)

Presentation Suggestions

Prepare areas of the classroom in advance for this activity. Arrange students in groups of three or four. Make sure that students label important buildings and other municipal sites. Students may also invent their own names for places, such as **El Museo Superfantástico**.

Assessment Opportunity

After groups have designed their plazas, have them create a simple set for a miniature theater. Have them invent a cast of characters and put on a skit that takes place in their plaza. If equipment is available, you may wish to videotape students performing. Students may be assessed according to how well they use what they have learned in **Unidad 9,** what they recycle from previous units, and their originality in creating the set and dialogue.

¡HABLEMOS! (pp. 196–197)

Presentation Suggestions

Have the class repeat the conversation and vocabulary after you or the Lesson Tape. Discuss the illustrations on p. 196. Have volunteers read the captions and try to figure out what the unfamiliar words mean from visual and context clues. What clues are in words such as **supermercado, zoológico, estadio, apartamentos?**

Re-enter/Recycle

Bring into your discussion other places in a city or town that students have previously learned—for example, **el rascacielos, el centro, la farmacia**. Ask heritage speakers if they can think of any other places in a city.

Toward Cultural Understanding

The following is a common structure for schools in Spanish-speaking countries:

1. **escuela primaria** (*elementary school*)
2. **colegio** (high school for students preparing to go to university)

   escuela normal (high school for students preparing to become teachers)

   escuela técnica (high school for technical careers in offices)

   liceo (a combination of junior high or middle school)
3. **universidad** (*university*)

PRACTIQUEMOS (pp. 198–199)

Presentation Suggestions

These activities can be done as classwork, homework, individual work, or pair work. Warm up by reviewing the vocabulary.

Photocopy the Vocabulary Cards from the *Resource and Activity Book* and distribute to students. Then ask **¿Hay un supermercado aquí?** Students holding a supermarket card should stand and say **Sí, hay un supermercado aquí.** Play variations of this game until all students have had a turn and all new vocabulary has been reviewed.

Cooperative Learning

Read to students the on-page note about Simón Bolívar. Then have students form groups to research two other Latin American heroes, Benito Juárez and José de San Martín, and find places named for them in Mexico and Argentina, respectively. Some students can look up information about these historical figures in encyclopedias and other reference books, while other students can research atlases for places named for them. Together the group can write a short biography about these people. Finally, they can make an oral report to the class.

Assessment Opportunity

Have students write three or four short sentences describing what they like to do on Saturdays. Have students work in small groups to read their lists and compare responses.

ENTRE AMIGOS (p. 200)

Re-enter/Recycle

Warm-up with a game of "¿Dónde está el borrador?" Review with students all the prepositions and location expressions they know and write them on the board. Have a student volunteer be **el (la) detective** *(detective)*, and send him or her outside the room while another student hides the chalkboard eraser. When the detective returns, classmates take turns giving him or her location clues until the eraser is found.

Presentation Suggestions

Read through the activity with students and make sure they all understand the directions. To make the activity easier, have students begin their map or sketch by placing something directly in the center, such as a plaza, park, or building. This can serve as the initial point of reference. Students may be helped with their dialogues if a few simple sentences are displayed on the chalkboard such as **Hay un/a _____ cerca. Está a la izquierda del museo.**

Enrichment

Encourage students to put **un puente** *(bridge)*, **una tienda** *(store)*, **un correo** *(post office)*, or other details in their sketches.

¿CÓMO LO DICES? (pp. 201–202)

Re-enter/Recycle

As a warm-up, ask students entering the class questions using **estar** such as: **¿Cómo estás? ¿Dónde estás? ¿Estás contento/a? ¿Estás hablando?** Have students answer before taking their seats: **Estoy en la clase. Sí, estoy contento.** Continue until all students have taken their seats.

Presentation Suggestions

This *¿Cómo lo dices?* provides a formal review of **estar**. Write the present tense forms of **estar**, without English translation, on the chalkboard. Have volunteers read the paragraph and answer the questions on p. 202.

Extension

Have students take turns making short sentences using a form of **estar**. Each student should use a different form of **estar** than was used by the student who went before. Students may use the vocabulary from the paragraph in *¿Cómo lo dices?* on p. 201.

¡ÚSALO! (pp. 203–205)

Presentation Suggestions

Read aloud the first sentence on p. 203 and ask a volunteer to help you model the conversation. Exercise A can be completed as classwork or pair work.

TPR

Call on volunteers to pantomime the action words on p. 203. Then have two students come to the front of the class and pantomime an action word together. Ask **¿Qué están haciendo?** and elicit the response **Están _____ .**

Enrichment

Have students select and cut out a newspaper photograph and paste it to a sheet of paper. Then have them write a real or fictional description of what is happening in the photograph. They should use forms of **estar** at least four times in their description.

ENTRE AMIGOS (p. 206)

Tap Background Knowledge

Ask students how much time they spend on the telephone. What are they most likely to use the phone for? What would their life be like if they could not use the phone? How do they feel about using the phone to practice Spanish?

Presentation Suggestions

Display a list of salutations and typical questions that are often asked on the phone. Tell students that it is normal to be tongue-tied in a phone conversation when speaking in a foreign language, especially if they are talking with a stranger. Learning a few formalities, however, can help relieve the awkwardness.

Language Across the Curriculum

Language Arts Although telephone conversations are something students take for granted, they may not realize that conducting even a simple phone conversation in a foreign language is hard because they are being deprived of visual clues that help them decode meaning. It takes much more concentration to speak over the phone than to talk to someone in person.

¿CÓMO LO DICES? (pp. 207–208)

Re-enter/Recycle

As a warm-up, ask simple rapid-fire questions using **tener** and classroom objects, eliciting a response with direct object pronouns and **tengo**. For example: **Paco, ¿tienes el libro? Sí, lo tengo.** Continue with similar questions that elicit answers with indirect object pronouns: **Aurora, ¿a quién das el libro? Le doy el libro a Jaime.**

Presentation Suggestion

Invite students to read the captions to the illustrations on p. 207, as well as the sample sentences on p. 208. Help them note the expressions that use infinitive forms. Point out to students that native speakers of Spanish use the direct and indirect object pronouns in both positions—preceding the verb phrase and connected to the infinitive—interchangeably. Neither is a preferred method.

Stress extensive oral practice of this section to accustom students to hearing the object pronouns used in both positions. You may wish to play the conversations on the Lesson Tape each day for students to hear other models of the construction in communication contexts.

Extension

Bring two beach balls or foam-rubber balls to class. Toss one ball to a student while saying what you are doing (e.g., **Le tiro la pelota a Rita.**). Have students continue accordingly. Students may also use the simpler phrase **Te la tiro.** Vary the activity by tossing balls to two students (e.g., **Les tiro las pelotas a José y a Enrique.**). Use this activity to review the use of direct and indirect object pronouns.

¡ÚSALO! (p. 209)

Presentation Suggestions

Read the instructions for both exercises and let pairs of students work together to complete them. All responses should be written. After students finish, ask for volunteers to tell the class what they have written. You may also wish to have students role-play their questions and answers for the class.

Re-enter/Recycle

You may wish to review prepositions in conjunction with Exercise A.

ENTRE AMIGOS (p. 210)

Presentation Suggestions

Make sure students understand the rules on p. 210 before you begin to play the game. Remind students that they are going to use direct object pronouns in their answers. Review these pronouns with the class and display them on the board.

Enrichment

To make the game more interesting you might want to incorporate some additional Spanish baseball vocabulary:

pitcher	**lanzador**
catcher	**receptor**
1st base	**primera base**
2nd base	**segunda base**
3rd base	**tercera base**
shortstop	**corto campo**
right field	**campo (jardín) derecho**
left field	**campo (jardín) izquierdo**
center field	**campo (jardín) central**
inning	**entrada**
umpire	**árbitro**
home run	**jonrón**

¡A DIVERTIRNOS! (p. 211)

Presentation Suggestions

If possible, bring Spanish-language comic books to class. Allow students to take turns looking at them to get ideas about how they might format their own comic strips.

UNIDAD 10
UNIT OVERVIEW

OBJECTIVES

Communicate

- Talk about the location of places
- Give directions to places
- Practice telling others politely what to do and what not to do

Build Vocabulary

- Describe places and where they are located with words such as **la cuadra, la esquina, norte, sur**
- Learn useful words and expressions for giving directions and getting around, such as **adelante, atrás, perderse, quedar, rápido, despacio**
- Learn measurements for distances such as **metro** and **kilómetro**

Structure the Language

- Use affirmative **tú** commands of regular **-ar, -er,** and **-ir** verbs
- Use **tú** commands with reflexive verbs
- Use negative **tú** commands such as **no hables, no comas,** etc.
- Form questions with the interrogative **¿a cuántos/as?**
- Use **quedar** to indicate location

Understand Culture

The cultural focus of **Unidad 10** is about getting around in Spanish-speaking cities.

Recycle

Unidad 10 offers opportunities to recycle the following language:

- Affirmative **tú** commands
- Prepositions of place: **delante de, detrás de**, and **cerca de**
- **Tener que** + infinitive

PROGRAM RESOURCES

- Workbook, pp. 123–134
- Overhead Transparencies 25, 26
- Lesson Tape **Unidad 10**, Exercise Tape **Unidad 10**
- Resource and Activity Book
    ¡Hablemos! Masters 26, 27
    Vocabulary Cards Masters 110–117
    Vocabulary Review Master 149
    ¡A conversar! Master 163
    Tape Exercise and Pronunciation
    Pages 23–24
- Culture Resource Book, Masters 20, 21
- Test Blackline Masters and Tape, **Unidad 10**

MATERIALS TO GATHER

- Road maps, encyclopedias, or atlases— several of each (*Entre amigos*, p. 217)
- Local maps of your neighborhood or town (*Entre amigos*, p. 221)
- Meter stick
- Compass

TRATEGIES

UNIT OPENER (pp. 212–213)

Tap Background Knowledge

Ask students about different problems they have encountered when giving or following directions. What do students do to avoid misunderstandings when giving or receiving directions in an unfamiliar place? Have students ever had to ask for or give directions to someone who didn't know their language? What did they do to make that easier?

The Heritage Speaker

If your class has heritage speakers who have recently come to the United States, invite them to tell about experiences they have had trying to understand directions in English. Can they give any advice on giving directions to someone who doesn't understand your language?

Language Across the Curriculum

Math Make sure students understand what the metric system is. Explain that when speaking Spanish, it is more appropriate to use the metric system than the English system. If possible, bring a meter stick to class—otherwise, you may approximate a meter by holding a pencil in each hand and stretching your arms outward. Remind students that a kilometer has 1,000 meters. Have students use a map key or legend to find out approximately how many kilometers are equal to one mile. (A mile is about 1.6 kilometers long.)

¡HABLEMOS! (pp. 214–215)

Tap Background Knowledge

Have the class locate the four cardinal directions. Use a compass, if available. What do students associate with each of the directions (e.g., geographical features, warmer or cooler weather)? What lies outside the school in each direction and how far away is it? Have the class make the most complete description they can of where the school is located. At the end of the unit, they should be able to give this description in Spanish.

Presentation Suggestions

Direct students' attention to the compass rose on p. 214. How many direction words are obvious from cognate clues? Some cognates are more obvious when they are spoken than when read. As you go through the vocabulary, remind students to always look for context clues for unfamiliar words.

The Multi-Level Class

Ask for volunteers to look around the classroom, close their eyes, and then tell from memory what is on the north wall, the east wall, and so on. Invite confident students to offer more elaborate descriptions, or tell of things outside the school. Afterward, you may call out the cardinal points one by one in Spanish and have the class point out which way that direction is.

Extension

In small groups, students should draw a map showing a route from school to a location you designate. Have them label their map using as much vocabulary from p. 214 as they can. Then they should compare their route with that of another group. Whose route is the shortest? Whose map is the most complete?

PRACTIQUEMOS (pp. 216–217)

Presentation Suggestions

Read aloud the English introduction and do Exercise A as classwork. Have students follow the models to say where they live, how far away their houses are from school, and in what direction—for example, **Mi casa está al oeste de la escuela.** Ask similar questions regarding other towns, cities, or states; or have volunteers make up questions for the class.

The Heritage Speaker

Invite heritage speakers to tell where they, their families, or their friends are from. Have them locate the towns or cities on a map and give directions explaining where they are from in relation to nearby cities or countries.

Listening Comprehension

Play a game in which you say where something is located, without telling the name of the place or thing, and students try to identify what you are referring to—for example: **Está a dos cuadras al norte de la escuela, en la esquina. ¿Qué es?**

Cooperative Learning

In groups of four, have one student describe in Spanish the location of a place in a city or town, including as much detail as possible.

The other students should draw a map showing what the first student has described, then show the map to the first student for correction. Students should then change roles and repeat the activity.

For the Nonspecialist

If students are interested, you may want to introduce the words for northwest (**noroeste**), northeast (**noreste**), southeast (**sudeste**), and southwest (**suroeste**).

ENTRE AMIGOS (p. 217)

Presentation Suggestions

Have a volunteer read the English instructions. Before dividing the class into pairs, explain to students that they will be studying the maps together with their partners. They will need to agree upon which cities to discuss, and make a list of things they want to ask questions about. Students should create at least five questions for their partners.

Extension

Find a map of your area that shows distances. Display the map in class and use it to ask questions about the distances between different points. You may have students express distances first in **millas** and then in **kilómetros**.

¡HABLEMOS! (pp. 218–219)

Presentation Suggestions

Students have already learned how to use the verb **quedar** with clothes (**me queda grande**). Point out that they can also use **quedar** to talk about the location of places. Model the conversation on p. 218 with a heritage speaker or play the Lesson Tape. Have pairs of volunteers read the conversation aloud. Finally, have other students read the conversation, but substituting appropriate alternatives for **señora, el almacén, atrás,** and **mi papá**.

Re-enter/Recycle

Review other expressions students have learned for giving locations such as **delante de, detrás de,** and **cerca de**.

Cooperative Learning

In small groups, students should discuss and write down what each person does **rápido** and **despacio**. Then one person from each group should read their list to the class—for example, **Ana siempre come rápido, pero camina muy despacio**.

Toward Cultural Understanding

In places such as San José, Costa Rica, it is very common for people to give directions and locations of places in terms of landmarks. For example, it would be common for you to hear that such and such a place is located **cuatrocientos metros al norte de la vieja farmacia**. As long as you know where the "old pharmacy" is, you're OK!

PRACTIQUEMOS (pp. 220–221)

Presentation Suggestions

Read the directions and the example for Exercise A. Then call on volunteers to answer the questions. Assign Exercise B for pair work or as a homework exercise.

Extension

Elicit from the class five more questions that José Zamora might ask about your city. Write

them on the board. Have the students get together in pairs and repeat Exercise B with the new questions.

Language Across the Curriculum

Mathematics/Science Display the word pairs kilometer/**kilómetro** and gram/**gramo**. Explain that the English and Spanish words used in the metric system tend to be very similar. Challenge students to guess the English or Spanish equivalents for the following words: **metro** *(meter)*, **litro** *(liter)*, **kilogramo** *(kilogram)*, **centímetro** *(centimeter)*.

ENTRE AMIGOS (p. 221)

Presentation Suggestions

Draw a simple gridlike street map on the board, including a compass rose and leaving plenty of space to draw. Have volunteers add something to the map, making sure to label it. When the map is finished, use it as the basis for questions, such as how one gets from one place to another, how far places are from each other, and where things are located.

Cooperative Learning

Have students work in groups of four or five to create more difficult questions, such as **¿A cuántas millas está la ciudad de la capital del estado?** Each student should work to research the information to a question, and then write a short answer of two to three sentences to create a descriptive narrative about their city in relation to other places. For example: **Albany, la capital de mi estado, está a ciento setenta millas de mi ciudad. La capital queda al norte de Nueva York.**

¿CÓMO LO DICES? (pp. 222–223)

Presentation Suggestions

Engage students with a rapid-fire list of affirmative **tú** commands: **Marcos, abre la puerta. Inés, lee el libro. Sonia, escribe una carta a tu mamá.** Discuss the various situations in which commands are used and demonstrate how tone and phrasing can alter the strength of a command. Review the chart of familiar commands on p. 222. Give students other regular verbs from which to make commands, such as **cantar, comer,** or **escribir**.

Re-enter/Recycle

Have students come up with non-command forms they already know that can be used to express implied commands. Remind them that a command can sometimes be phrased more gently in the form of a question. Have them produce examples. **(Tienes que hacer la tarea. ¿Puedes leer la carta?)**

Assessment Opportunity

Take students to the gymnasium or another open, uncluttered area, and have them practice giving commands to one another, alternating between affirmative and negative familiar commands.

The Multi-Level Class

At this point, all students should be familiar with constructing simple **tú** commands. Provide a situation, such as "Your little brother took your homework." Then ask students for appropriate commands. Advanced students should answer using more than one verb or explaining the reason for their demand by using **porque**.

Extension

In small groups, each student should take a turn playing the role of the parent and give appropriate commands to another member who will play a child. Students should pantomime responses to the commands.

¡ÚSALO! (pp. 223–225)

Presentation Suggestions

Point out that commands frequently involve an object—for example, **Trae el libro**. Point to various objects around the classroom and ask students to come up with commands that relate to each. Have a volunteer read the instructions for each of the exercises. The exercises may be done as classwork or homework.

Re-enter/Recycle

Have students name the different rooms in an imaginary house and then list the commands that would commonly be used in each room. You might add to the context by offering an object for each room. For example: **el dormitorio, la ropa—Recoge la ropa (del piso)**.

The Heritage Speaker

Heritage speakers may wish to share with the class some commands that they hear at home, giving explanations for verbs that the class has not yet learned.

TPR

Have each student write a command on a piece of paper. Students should then exchange pieces of paper with their neighbors and, one by one, pantomime responses to the command they have received. The class should guess from each student's response what the command was.

ENTRE AMIGOS (p. 225)

Presentation Suggestions

As a warm-up, play a game of "Simón dice…" as a class. Possible script:

> **Simón dice: Levántate.**
>
> **Simón dice: Canta una canción.**
>
> **Simón dice: Siéntate.**
>
> **Pon la mano en el escritorio.**
>
> **¡Ay, no! ¡Tengo que decir: Simón dice!**

¿CÓMO LO DICES? (pp. 226–227)

Presentation Suggestions

Read the introduction and then have pairs of volunteers read aloud the sample conversations on p. 226. Ask students to point out the new construction of the negative command. Review the chart on p. 227 and give students other verbs from which to make negative commands, such as **bailar, vivir, abrir,** or **beber. (No bailes, no vivas, no abras, no bebas.)**

The Multi-Level Class

When all students have some proficiency constructing simple negative **tú** commands, have students create negative commands from the infinitive form of verbs. For example, **comer: ¡No comas!** Advanced students should answer with longer sentences—for example, **¡No comas mi manzana porque tengo mucha hambre!**

Extension

Have the class imagine they are in a science class laboratory. Have them create a list of five to ten rules of behavior in the form of negative commands.

¡ÚSALO! (pp. 228–229)

Presentation Suggestions

Point out that negative commands are sometimes used to stop someone from doing something that is inadvisable. Sometimes they are used just to stop someone from doing something you don't like them to do. Have students list things that they don't like other people to do. Then have them produce appropriate negative commands. For example, **hablar en voz alta: No hables en voz alta.**

Critical Thinking

Have students create warning signs or signs with the circle-and-slash symbol over an activity or object. Have them trade signs and write (on a separate piece of paper) a negative command that describes the sentiment of the sign they received.

Extension

After finishing Exercise C, have students produce at least one other rule for each of the six locations mentioned.

Toward Cultural Understanding

Explain that different cultures use different gestures and body language to express the same message. In many Hispanic countries, a person will wave a finger from side to side to indicate that a person should not do something, while in the United States, people tend to shake a finger at the other person to convey the same point.

ENTRE AMIGOS (p. 230)

Presentation Suggestions

Ask students where they go for advice. To family? friends? school counselors? What constitutes good advice? bad advice? Ask for volunteers to share with the class examples of advice they have received in the past.

Critical Thinking

After finishing the activity, have students read aloud one rule or piece of advice. Compare and evaluate students' advice and make a list of the advice that the whole class agrees is good.

¡A DIVERTIRNOS! (p. 231)

Presentation Suggestions

Elicit from the class as many popular sayings as possible, and write them on the board. As a class, rephrase them in straightforward English and then discuss the differences between their actual and their literal meanings. Point out that poetic or exaggerated wording serves various functions. It increases the saying's impact and makes it more memorable. Explain that the same is true with Spanish sayings.

Extension

Have students show their posters to the class and see whether the class can correctly identify the sayings being illustrated.

Assessment Opportunity

You may wish to have students add their posters, or a description of them, to their portfolios.

The Heritage Speaker

Invite heritage Spanish speakers to share with the class additional sayings they know. They may wish to ask a Spanish-speaking parent or grandparent to help make a list of sayings and to find out in what circumstances the sayings are used. Ask the heritage speaker to help the rest of the class to understand what the sayings mean and how they are used.

UNIDAD 11
UNIT OVERVIEW

OBJECTIVES

Communicate

- Name people, places, and things related to shopping
- Talk about buying gifts
- Talk about things that happened in the past

Build Vocabulary

- Name people and things found in jewelry stores, such as **el joyero, el collar, el brazalete**
- Name people and things found in shoe stores, such as **el zapatero, las sandalias, el cinturón**
- Name things found in music stores, such as **el disco compacto, el casete, el disco**

Structure the Language

- Use singular and plural past forms of regular **-ar** verbs
- Learn about spelling changes in the first-person past forms of verbs like **pagar, almorzar, jugar, sacar**

Understand Culture

The cultural focus of **Unidad 11** is on shopping in Spain and Latin America, and on gift items for which certain Spanish-speaking countries are known.

Recycle

Unidad 11 offers opportunities to recycle the following language:

- Numbers
- Indirect object pronouns
- Language related to money and spending
- Affirmative and negative commands

PROGRAM RESOURCES

- Workbook, pp. 135–146
- Overhead Transparencies 27, 28
- Lesson Tape **Unidad 11**, Exercise Tape **Unidad 11**
- Resource and Activity Book

    ¡Hablemos! Masters 28, 29
    Vocabulary Cards Masters 118–126
    Vocabulary Review Masters 150, 151
    ¡A conversar! Master 164
    Tape Exercise and Pronunciation Pages 25–26

- Culture Resource Book, Masters 22, 23–24
- Test Blackline Masters and Tape, **Unidad 11**

MATERIALS TO GATHER

- Cardboard, scissors, toothpicks; index cards (*¡A divertirnos!*, p. 253)
- Costume jewelry, play money (optional)
- Newspaper advertisements for jewelry, shoe, and/or record stores

STRATEGIES

UNIT OPENER (pp. 232–233)

Presentation Suggestions

Using props, such as articles of clothing and play money, engage volunteers in mock bargaining. When students understand how bargaining is done, have them bargain with each other.

Toward Cultural Understanding

After reading the *¿Sabes que...?* feature, you may wish to share the following with students:

Open-air markets are very common in Spanish-speaking countries. Towns often have a market that takes place one day a week. Larger cities have several markets, in different locations and on different days of the week, to service the various neighborhoods. Some markets specialize in one kind of merchandise, such as produce or homemade crafts.

Bargaining is an important part of some Spanish-speaking cultures. Not all haggling results in a reduced price. Sometimes the customer can talk the vendor into including another item for free with the purchase.

The livelihood of some small Latin American villages depends heavily on crafts—for example, blankets, shawls, or works of art—that its people make and then sell in local markets.

The Heritage Speaker

Invite heritage speakers to share with the class what they know about shopping practices, markets, malls, and stores in their countries of origin. Ask them to comment on similarities or differences between their experiences in their home countries with what they see in the photographs. What are the current fashions for kids in their home towns or cities? Ask if they know of products or crafts for which their countries are well known.

¡HABLEMOS! (pp. 234–235)

Presentation Suggestions

Have the class repeat the conversations and vocabulary after you or the Lesson Tape. Call on pairs of volunteers to role-play the conversations with their books open. Have them substitute various jewelry items, such **los llaveros** or **los brazaletes**. Supply one- or two-word cues for the item you want them to substitute.

TPR

Using jewelry-store props, lead individuals through TPR command strings. For example, **Estela, muéstrame el brazalete. Tócalo. Levántalo. Ponlo sobre la mesa. Ahora levanta el collar. Póntelo. Mírate en el espejo.**

The Multi-Level Class

Challenge heritage speakers and more proficient students to make up their own TPR command phrases similar to the ones above. Check their work. Then call on volunteers to work with heritage students. Have students go through each command phrase at least three times or until the meaning is clear to the rest of the class.

Language Across the Curriculum

History After reading *Así es...*, remind students that the search for gold was one of the driving forces behind Spain's colonization of the New

World. Using indigenous slaves, the Spanish extracted thousands of tons of gold and silver from mines in Latin America, and sent it back to Europe. Gold and silver mines still exist in many countries, such as Peru and Mexico, though they are very depleted after centuries of mining.

PRACTIQUEMOS (p. 236)

Presentation Suggestions

If possible, use props to present this activity. Lay the props out on a table. Pick up the bracelet and say the model sentence. Pick up the other items one by one and ask for volunteers to make the substitution. Then invite other volunteers to come to the table to pick up items one by one and say the appropriate sentence.

ENTRE AMIGOS (p. 237)

Presentation Suggestions

In large classes, have students work together in groups, rather than individually, to arrive at a guess for each item. To ask the different groups what their guesses were for each item, say **¿Qué creen ustedes?** OR **¿Qué piensan ustedes?** In doing the activity, tell students to count as a "jewel" any stone that is part of a bracelet, necklace, or ring.

For the Nonspecialist

Use **llevar** for items that are worn: **¿Cuántos alumnos llevan brazalete?** Use **tener** for the items that students don't wear but have with them: **¿Cuántos alumnos tienen joyas?**

Language Across the Curriculum

Math When creating your class bar graph, conduct a mini-lesson on graphing. Point out and name the X-axis and Y-axis, and leave plenty of space between each bar. Explain that a bar graph is useful for comparing and illustrating sizes or quantities.

¡HABLEMOS! (pp. 238–239)

Presentation Suggestions

Have the class repeat the conversations and vocabulary after you or the Lesson Tape.

For further practice with the conversations, assume the role of the first speaker in the conversation. Circulate and designate individuals to assume the role of the second speaker. After four or five such role-plays, challenge more proficient students to assume the role with their books closed.

Re-enter/Recycle

Use all previously learned vocabulary to recycle the use of direct and indirect object pronouns. Distribute Vocabulary Cards from the *Resource and Activity Book* to students. Explain that each item is a gift for someone else. Then use the following model and substitute different items:

T: **¿Quién tiene las sandalias?**

S1: **Yo tengo las sandalias.** OR **Yo las tengo.**

T: **¿A quién le vas a dar las sandalias?**

S1: **Voy a darle las sandalias a mi hermana.**

Toward Cultural Understanding

After reading *Así es...*, you may wish to share with students that people who live in cities and towns in Spanish-speaking countries often pay more attention to fashion than many people do in the United States. Although ready-to-wear clothing is available, many people still search fashion magazines for pictures of the styles of clothing they want **modistas** *(seamstresses)* and **sastres** *(tailors)* to make so that a dress, suit, and accessories are **a la última moda** *(in the latest style)*.

Listening Comprehension

Once the unit vocabulary has been introduced and practiced, mention items from each of the stores and have individual students respond by saying the kind of store where the item is found.

PRACTIQUEMOS (pp. 240–241)

Re-enter/Recycle

Make a transparency of a map that students prepared for **Unidad 10** and use it to practice affirmative and negative commands. Use an erasable marker for students to trace their route from one place to another according to your commands. To vary the activity, have one student be the "driver" and another the "navigator." If the person giving directions hesitates, encourage the driver to ask questions—for example: **¿Qué hago? ¿Doblo a la derecha o a la izquierda?**

Presentation Suggestions

Call on individual students to complete the items in Exercise A. After students have completed the activity, have them role-play the situation, using vocabulary cards or real items. Encourage students to use direct pronouns whenever possible. For Exercise B, encourage students to change roles during the activity.

Critical Thinking

After students complete Exercise C, have them bring to class pages with advertisements from newspapers or magazines. The class can decide which items are **barato** and which are **caro**.

Extension

Review the verb **costar**, and have one student be a salesclerk and another a customer. They may act out the parts using the following model:

S1: **¿Cuánto cuesta el disco?**

S2: **El disco cuesta diez dólares.**

S1: **¡Diez dólares! ¡Es muy caro!**

ENTRE AMIGOS (p. 242)

Presentation Suggestions

To prepare students for the activity, ask additional questions similar to those in the example about other stores on the sample map. Focus on map skills by asking how to get from one point to another on the map. For example: **Estoy en la zapatería. ¿Cómo voy a la tienda de discos?**

¿CÓMO LO DICES? (pp. 243–244)

Presentation Suggestions

Invite volunteers to read parts of the English presentation aloud while the rest of the class reads along silently. To explain the meaning of the first two examples, point out the calendar pages in the pictures and explain that in each instance someone is thinking about something that happened the day before.

Go over the verb chart with students. Call on different students to tell you what the endings are for the past tense.

Extension

Point to the preceding day's date on the calendar. Ask questions such as the following:

1. **¿Hablaste con tus amigos ayer?**
2. **¿Compraste algo ayer?**
3. **¿Adónde caminaste ayer?**
4. **¿Qué estudiaste ayer?**
5. **¿Tomaste el desayuno ayer?**

After students gain confidence, have them elaborate on their answers—for example: **Sí, hablé con Juan y María ayer. Hablamos una hora.**

Enrichment

Play "El ahorcado" (see "Games and Activities" in this *Teacher's Edition*) to practice **-ar** verbs with spelling changes in the past tense.

¡ÚSALO! (pp. 245–246)

Presentation Suggestions

Set aside class time for students to complete Exercise A individually. As an alternative to assigning Exercise B as pair work, assume the role of the questioner and have individuals supply the answers. After students have completed Exercise C in pairs, have them compare their answers as a class activity.

Extension

After students have completed Exercise B, have them ask you the same questions to practice the **usted** form.

The Multi-Level Class

Have students write a paragraph about gifts they received for their birthdays or a holiday. Give them the verb **regalar** and remind them to consult the charts in the textbook if they do not remember a verb form. Encourage students to decorate their paragraphs with color drawings of their gifts. Call on more proficient students to read their paragraphs to the class.

ENTRE AMIGOS (p. 247)

Presentation Suggestions

As a warm-up to the activity, ask students what they did last week. Encourage them to supply as many details as possible. As students mention different activities, you may want to list or cluster them on the board, so that the class can refer to the list while they create and discuss their schedules.

¿CÓMO LO DICES? (pp. 248–249)

Presentation Suggestions

You may wish to explain the spelling change in the **yo** form of **pagar** by writing the word **general** on the board and using it to demonstrate the pronunciation of **ge**. Contrast the **ge** in **general** with the **gue** in **pagué.**

After you have modeled each pronunciation, have volunteers take turns pronouncing them. Point out that the use of **c** in **almorcé** is similar to the change of **lápiz** to **lápices.**

Re-enter/Recycle

You may remind students of the verb **colgar** from *¿Qué tal?* Have them write the conjugation for the verb **colgar** on the chalkboard. Reiterate that many of the spelling changes in Spanish result from rules of pronunciation.

¡ÚSALO! (pp. 250–251)

Presentation Suggestions

Exercise A can be done individually or in pairs. Exercises B and C can be assigned for independent practice or completed as a whole-class activity. After students complete Exercise D in pairs, check for understanding by asking questions of individuals chosen at random.

Extension

After students have completed Exercise A, have them pretend that it was "Julio" who was sick and ask one another about what he did—for example, **¿A qué jugó Julio todas las tardes?**

After students have completed Exercise B, you may wish to use the story sentences for dictation practice. Have students exchange papers to correct spelling, paying close attention to the verb forms.

For the Nonspecialist

Note that past forms for reflexive verbs are the same as for nonreflexive ones. Reflexive pronouns appear before the verb in the sentence (e.g., **Me cepillé los dientes. Me bañé.**).

Assessment Opportunity

After students have completed the exercises for this unit, check for understanding and reinforce learning by giving students exercises from previous units or levels that use regular -ar verbs in the present tense and having them rework the exercises, changing the verbs to the past tense.

ENTRE AMIGOS (p. 252)

Presentation Suggestions

If some students haven't visited the stores suggested in the activity, have them tell about a visit to some other type of store. Visits to cinemas, the theater, or museums will also work for this activity as long as they allow students to practice the past tense forms of regular **-ar** verbs. You may wish to demonstrate note-taking techniques before pairs work together. Explain to students that they only need to write the name of the place and what their partner bought.

¡A DIVERTIRNOS! (p. 253)

Presentation Suggestions

If necessary, lead students through a step-by-step sequence for constructing their spinners. You may wish to elicit a few examples for each of the four categories from the class and cluster them on the board to help students get started.

UNIDAD 12
UNIT OVERVIEW

OBJECTIVES

Communicate

- Name beach and water sports
- Describe beach activities and name items related to the beach
- Talk about past actions
- Talk about things that are near and far away

Build Vocabulary

- Name beach and water activities and related words such as **tomar el sol, la crema de broncear, la sombrilla, la arena, flotar, la lancha**
- Describe people with adjectives such as **bronceada** and **quemada**
- Name water sports such as **el esquí acuático**

Structure the Language

- Talk about past actions using the past tense of **-er** and **-ir** verbs
- Use the demonstrative adjectives to talk about people and things that are near and far
- Use the preposition **para** in different ways

Understand Culture

The cultural focus of **Unidad 12** is on popular beach activities and famous beach areas in Spanish-speaking countries.

Recycle

Unidad 12 offers opportunities to recycle the following language:

- Sentences with **gustar, querer, saber,** and **tener que**
- Reflexives
- Time expressions
- Informal commands

PROGRAM RESOURCES

- Workbook, pp. 147–158
- Overhead Transparencies 29, 30
- Lesson Tape **Unidad 12**, Exercise Tape **Unidad 12**
- Resource and Activity Book
    ¡Hablemos! Masters 30, 31
    Vocabulary Cards Masters 127–135
    Vocabulary Review Masters 152, 153
    ¡A conversar! Master 165
    Tape Exercise and Pronunciation Pages 27–29
- Culture Resource Book, Masters 25, 26, 27
- Test Blackline Masters and Tape, **Unidad 12**

MATERIALS TO GATHER

- 3" x 5" cards (*Entre amigos*, p. 259)
- Brochures or magazines with pictures of beach destinations (*Entre amigos*, p. 263)
- Poster board
- Photographs, stiff paper, and binding materials to make a "photo essay book" (*¡A divertirnos!*, p. 275)

STRATEGIES

UNIT OPENER (pp. 254–255)

Tap Background Knowledge

To help introduce the theme of the unit, join the class in talking about water sports and other beach activities. Have students work together to come up with as many Spanish words and expressions related to this theme as they can—for example, **la playa, el agua, el sol, la toalla, jugar a,** and **ir de pesca**. Ask volunteers to use the words and expressions in sentences pertaining to beach activities. Tell the class about time you've spent at the beach, using Spanish that students understand, if possible. Invite heritage speakers to do the same.

Presentation Suggestions

Point out the photographs and have students examine them. Then call on volunteers to use Spanish to identify different aspects or things in the photographs. After students have read *¿Sabes que...?*, ask them what they think **La Costa Brava** means in English (*Fierce Coast*). Have students use a map or globe to locate Spain's Mediterranean coast, La Costa Brava, the Pacific coast of Mexico, and Acapulco.

The Heritage Speaker

Invite heritage speakers to explain what people do when they go to the beach in their home countries. Encourage their classmates to ask questions.

Language Across the Curriculum

Physical Education Have the class name different games and activities that are played or done at the beach or in the water. Discuss what kind of exercise is involved in each activity, including the benefits and any possible risks.

Critical Thinking

Read the *¿Sabes que...?* information about the cliff divers of Acapulco. Ask the class about this and other dangerous or risky sports. Have them name such sports and talk about why people engage in them. Find out from heritage speakers if high-risk sports are popular in their countries of origin, and if so, to tell about those activities.

¡HABLEMOS! (pp. 256–257)

Presentation Suggestions

To check for comprehension of the title, go around the room and ask different students the question **¿Qué haces en la playa?** Have students refer to the pictures as you call on different class members to describe what they see. Have them use Spanish as much as possible.

Invite two of the more proficient students to model the two conversations on these pages. You can also play them on the Lesson Tape. Then have pairs of students practice the conversation on p. 256, substituting items from this lesson or other appropriate items they know.

Re-enter/Recycle

This is a good opportunity to review the use of the verb **gustar**. Ask several students to answer the question **¿Qué te gusta hacer en la playa?** Then ask other class members to report what they said: **A Marta le gusta tomar el sol en la playa. A ellas les gustan nadar y descansar.**

Language Across the Curriculum

Geography Have students locate Costa Rica on a map or globe. Ask them to look in an encyclopedia or atlas to find out about Costa Rica's Pacific coast, especially its ocean currents. Have them relate what they find out to the information in the *Así es...* section.

PRACTIQUEMOS (pp. 258–259)

Presentation Suggestions

Have students take turns playing each role in Exercise A. Ask students to individually complete the sentences in Exercise B, writing their answers on a piece of paper. Then have students work with a partner to compare answers. You may wish to call on different students to tell the class what their completed sentences are. This exercise may be used for dictation practice on subsequent days.

Extension

Have students practice using the vocabulary on p. 258, using the following conversation as a model:

S1: **¿Qué vas a traer a la playa?**

S2: **Voy a traer la crema de broncear.**

Assessment Opportunity

Circulate around the room and listen in as students practice the Extension activity. Make notes on pronunciation problems for later practice with the entire class. Pay particular attention to students' pronunciation of **traer**, since the diphthong **ae** is difficult for students to master.

TPR

Introduce the command form **¡Tráeme...!** Then have students use Vocabulary Cards (*Resource and Activity Book*) to follow your commands—for example: **¡(Student's name) tráeme un salvavidas, por favor!**

ENTRE AMIGOS (p. 259)

Presentation Suggestions

Go over the instructions with students. Hand out 3" x 5" cards for students to use. To provide a model, write some partial sentences on the board. For example:

> **Querido/a _____,**
>
> **Estoy en la costa pacífica de _____.**
>
> **Me gusta _____.**

Extension

Have students draw pictures of the beach they're visiting on the reverse side of the cards you handed out. Then have them share their pictures with classmates. Alternatively, have students exchange postcards with a partner. Tell the pairs to take turns describing the beach scene as their partner draws it on the blank side of the postcard. Then have the partners comment on the drawings.

¡HABLEMOS! (pp. 260–261)

Presentation Suggestions

Model the conversations with a heritage speaker or play them on the Lesson Tape. Then have students move around the classroom and practice the conversations with different classmates. Join in the conversations as you check their work.

Language Across the Curriculum

Geography Have students use a map or globe to locate the countries mentioned in *Así es....* Then have students point out different coastal cities in the three countries. Ask heritage speakers to describe any of those countries they are familiar with. Heritage students may also be willing to talk about the dishes mentioned in the *Así es....*

Enrichment

In addition to the Spanish terms found in the on-page notes, Spanish-speakers have found it convenient to borrow English terms for some water activities. You often hear Spanish-speakers refer to surfing as **el surfing**, and to windsurfing as **el windsurf**. To show how English has borrowed words from Spanish, have students look up terms related to the rodeo.

PRACTIQUEMOS (p. 262)

Presentation Suggestions

If necessary, review the verb constructions in each activity item before students begin.

When students finish the activity, call on different class members to write the completed sentences on the board.

Extension

Ask students information questions about Juan and Julia. For example:

T: **¿Qué quiere buscar Juan?**

S: **Él quiere buscar conchas.**

T: **¿Quién sabe bucear muy bien?**

S: **Julia sabe bucear muy bien.**

ENTRE AMIGOS (p. 263)

Presentation Suggestions

Review the familiar command form of verbs with the class. Point out the use of **¡Toma...y toca...!** in the sample headline. You can have the students make drawings or cut out magazine pictures or scenes from travel brochures to use on their posters. As students prepare their posters, walk around the room answering questions and giving suggestions, as needed. Have students describe their posters as they present them. Encourage other students in the class to ask questions. When the groups finish their presentations, display the posters around the classroom for the entire class to enjoy.

Cooperative Learning

Spread more proficient speakers and heritage speakers among the different groups. Have groups divide the tasks, so that some students concentrate on collecting pictures, cutting them out and designing the poster, while others focus on developing ideas for the text of the poster.

Language Across the Curriculum

Visual Arts Have group members share ideas about the artistic merits of each other's posters. You may also wish to invite a visual arts teacher to come to class to comment on the posters.

¿CÓMO LO DICES? (pp. 264–265)

Presentation Suggestions

Review the pronunciation of past tense endings for **-ar** verbs. Go over the verb charts on pp. 264–265 with students. Ask different students to tell the class what endings are added to the verb stems to make the past tense. Call on more proficient students and ask them if they can form the past tense of some other regular **-er** and **-ir** verbs they have studied. Give them a verb form in the present tense and ask them to respond with the same verb form in the past tense. Do the same thing for several **o** to **ue** stem-changing verbs. You may consider working with **-er** verbs on one day and **-ir** verbs on the next.

Extension

To add context to the patterns presented here, have students work individually or in small groups to make up sentences for each of the verbs in the past tense. Provide examples such as **Yo corrí mucho en la playa ayer. Mis amigos salieron de mi casa a las nueve de la noche.** When students finish, have them share and compare their sentences with classmates. Ask them to write the sentences on the board for you to check.

For the Nonspecialist

The **vosotros/as** forms of the verbs presented here are **corristeis, salisteis,** and **volvisteis**.

¡ÚSALO! (pp. 265–266)

Presentation Suggestions

Assign different students the names from Exercise A before you call on them to answer the questions. Then ask different students the same questions using their own Spanish names.

Have different students write their completed Exercise B sentences on the board for you to check.

Give students sufficient time to make up their five sentences in Exercise C. If any students are having difficulty, you may write some useful sentence starters on the board. Invite students to move around the room to conduct their interviews. Tell students to use their imaginations when answering the questions. Circulate around the room as students conduct their interviews, noting correct question formation and correct use of the past tense in general.

Re-enter/Recycle

Review reflexive forms by having students identify the reflexives in Exercises B and C: **perderse, quedarme,** and **se perdieron**.

You can also review time expressions in these exercises: **a las ocho, a las nueve y media,** etc.

¿CÓMO LO DICES? (pp. 267–268)

Presentation Suggestions

Demonstrate the use of the demonstrative adjectives by selecting six students to mime the different situations and actions in the model sentences. Have them do so at different distances from you so that you can say each model sentence as you refer to a different student. For example, you say **Esta chica sabe nadar bien** as you point to a female student pretending to swim next to you.

Enrichment

Use classroom items to demonstrate the meanings of the demonstrative adjectives. You may also go for a walk with students and talk about the houses on the street or the parked cars, etc., using the demonstrative adjectives. For example: **Esta casa está muy cerca de nosotros. Esa casa está más lejos de nosotros. Aquella casa blanca está muy lejos de nosotros.**

¡ÚSALO! (pp. 268–269)

Presentation Suggestions

As much as possible, use gestures and place pictures or realia in different locations in the classroom to demonstrate the demonstrative adjectives as you or student volunteers read aloud answers to the various exercise items. Model Exercise C with a heritage speaker or a more proficient student. You may need to explain to students that the size of each item relates to its distance from the speakers (i.e., the smallest items are the farthest away).

Cooperative Learning

Have students work together in groups to make up and act out conversations of their own similar to those in Exercise C. Pair more proficient speakers with less proficient ones. Invite groups to present their conversations to the class.

ENTRE AMIGOS (p. 270)

Presentation Suggestions

After the groups have laid out their pictures, you may want to demonstrate a sample conversation with a heritage speaker as both of you stand at the table.

¿CÓMO LO DICES? (p. 271)

Presentation Suggestions

Answer any questions about the use of **para** and about the vocabulary and structures in the Spanish sentences. On the board, write the three uses of **para** as stated in the book. Label each as "A," "B," or "C." Then read aloud the Spanish sentences and have students assign the appropriate letter to each sentence.

Extension

You may wish to practice and reinforce each use of **para** separately by giving numerous examples and having volunteers answer questions based on your examples. Write some of the examples on the chalkboard and have students describe how **para** is used in each example.

¡ÚSALO! (pp. 272–273)

Presentation Suggestions

Tell students that for each activity they must pretend that they are the character who is answering the questions—in A: Carolina; in B: Paquito's brother. When students finish the activity, have them identify each use of **para** according to the statements you put on the board for *¿Cómo lo dices?* on p. 271.

ENTRE AMIGOS (p. 274)

Presentation Suggestions

Have students use the title of the article to guess what it is about. Then have them scan the article and guess again. Help students understand any unfamiliar vocabulary or structures in the article. Remind students that they do not have to understand every word in order to understand the main idea and important points about the article. Ask them to write yes/no and information questions about the content of the article. You may want to put an example of each kind of question on the board:

> ¿El *Nuestra Señora de Atocha* se perdió durante un huracán en 1973? (No.)

> ¿Qué encontraron los españoles cuando llegaron a América? (Encontraron oro, plata, perlas, y piedras preciosas.)

Toward Cultural Understanding

Students may be interested in learning of the history behind the *Atocha* story. The Spanish explorers did not go to the New World to seek religious freedom or to establish colonies. Their main interest centered on taking back to Spain all the riches they could find. The *Atocha* was just one of many treasure ships that never returned to home port. The wreckage of *Nuestra Señora de Atocha* was first discovered in 1973 by Mel Fisher after a great deal of archival detective work and careful searching off the Florida Keys. Although its discovery revealed millions of dollars' worth of treasure, the real treasure is the glimpse of life in the seventeenth century gained through studying the artifacts.

Listening Comprehension

Read the article aloud at least twice. Then have students answer questions like the samples above. You can also make up multiple choice questions for students to answer. For example,

Según el artículo, el verdadero tesoro del *Atocha* es:

   a) **un barco lleno de millones de dólares.**

   b) **el descubrimiento de oro y plata.**

   c) **información sobre la historia de las Américas.**

¡A DIVERTIRNOS! (p. 275)

Extension

Have students contribute to a wall display. Tell them to work in small groups to brainstorm about how they will keep up and use the Spanish they've learned in this course. Help them make up sentences from their ideas. Provide an example: **Voy a mirar un programa de televisión en español. Luego voy a llamar a mi amigo Pablo por teléfono. En español, voy a contarle algo sobre el programa.**

Next have students illustrate their sentences with drawings or pictures from magazines. Have them mount the illustrations alongside their sentences on poster board. Finally, display all the posters on a wall in the classroom.

RESOURCE SECTIONS

GAMES AND ACTIVITIES

In this resource section, you will find complete instructions for preparing and playing games and conducting activities that correspond to the instructional units in *¡Adelante!* The games and activities are listed alphabetically and contain the following information:

- **Materials.** A complete list of materials needed for the game or activity, including blackline masters of the *Resource and Activity Book*.

- **Players.** The number of students who can participate: specifically, the entire class, large groups (8–10 players), medium-size groups (5–8 players), small groups (3–5 players), and pairs.

- **Preparation.** Instructions for preparing materials in advance, as well as additional vocabulary, demonstrations, or explanations that may be needed before students begin.

- **Procedure.** A step-by-step description of how to play the game or conduct the activity.

The games and activities described here are merely suggestions. You should supplement and alter them according to your teaching situation. It is recommended, however, that you incorporate as many different games and activities as possible in your multisection class period to maintain a lively and interesting classroom atmosphere and provide meaningful practice in using Spanish.

For ease of selection, the games and activities in this resource section are coded with symbols to designate levels of difficulty:

O Lowest level of difficulty

◑ Average level of difficulty

● Highest level of difficulty

The following games and activities are included in this resource section:

1. Adivina el precio
2. El ahorcado
3. Antónimos
4. Busco la fortuna
5. La carta
6. Cinco
7. Completa la categoría
8. Concentración
9. Conquista el mundo
10. ¿Cuánto cuesta la palabra?
11. Descripciones I
12. Descripciones II
13. Dibujitos
14. ¿Dónde estoy?
15. Escoge tu número
16. El maratón
17. Pasapalabra
18. ¿Quién tiene la culpa?
19. Vamos en taxi
20. ¿Verdad o mentira?
21. El volcán

○ Adivina el precio

Materials
- Vocabulary cards of objects *(Resource and Activity Book)*
- Removable, self-adhesive notes 1¹/₂" x 2" or 3" x 3"

Players
The entire class or a medium-size to large group.

Preparation
Designate two or three students as "pricers," and help them assign a dollar value to each of the various items pictured on the vocabulary cards. Then have them write the prices on the self-adhesive notes and stick them to the backs of the appropriate vocabulary cards.

Procedure
The "pricers" announce each item as it comes up for bid. They then choose three "contestants" from the class, each of whom gets just one chance to guess the price of the item as indicated on the back of the card. The contestant who comes closest to the price without going over wins a point. The contestant with the most points after three items have been up for bid wins that round and gets to take the place of one of the "pricers." The game continues until everyone has had a chance to be either a pricer or a contestant.

○ El ahorcado

Materials
- Chalkboard and chalk or pencil and paper

Players
The entire class, or students working in pairs or small groups.

Preparation
None

Procedure
Play "Hangman" in Spanish. One person chooses a Spanish word, such as a verb form, and draws lines for the number of letters. The partner guesses the letters of the alphabet (if possible, in Spanish). For each incorrect guess, a part of a figure is drawn. If the figure is complete before the word is guessed, the person who chose the word wins. If not, the person guessing wins.

For review, you may specify that students use prepositions, verbs, or adjectives for their words.

◑ Antónimos

Materials
- 3" x 3" squares of paper or index cards
- Paper bag

Players Students playing in pairs.

Preparation Make (or have students make) game cards by folding each of several squares of paper in half and then folding it in half once more. On the inner halves, write antonym pairs (e.g., **llegar–salir, subir–bajar, pagar–recibir, dentro de–fuera de, cerca–lejos**), making sure that one antonym is on one side of the fold and its opposite on the other. Make a set of ten antonym pairs for each pair of students. Then put each set into a colorful paper shopping or gift bag and shake well.

Procedure Have students choose partners and give each pair of players a bag. The first player draws a slip of paper from the bag, opens it up, and reads one of the words. The second player must not only pronounce its antonym correctly but also spell it correctly. If successful, the player keeps the antonym pair. If not, he or she returns it to the bag.

The bag is then shaken up before the second player draws a game card. The player who collects the most antonym pairs wins the game.

● Busco la fortuna

Materials
- Transparency and overhead projector (or the chalkboard and chalk or a large piece of paper and a marking pen)
- 4" x 6" index cards
- Play money

Players The entire class or a medium-size to large group.

Preparation	On the transparency, chalkboard, or paper, draw dashed lines to stand for the letters of a familiar expression (e.g., **Estoy muy bien. ¡Buena suerte! Mejor tarde que nunca.).** On the index cards, write large amounts of money (or amounts that correspond to the numbers students have learned); shuffle the cards and place them face down on a table. To make the game more interesting, you may add cards such as "lose a turn" **(pierde un turno)**, "free spin" **(turno extra)** or "bankrupt" **(bancarrota)**. Either make or purchase play money for the winnings.
Procedure	Divide the class into teams. One team chooses an index card. If a money amount is on the card, the team gets to guess a consonant in the expression. If the guess is correct, write the consonant on the dashed line(s) where it appears in the expression. Then give the team the matching amount of play money. The team continues playing until it either turns up a bad card (e.g., **bancarrota)** or does not guess a letter correctly. If a team has enough money, it may buy a vowel for an agreed-upon price **(Quiero comprar una vocal.).**
	A team may try to guess the expression after it has completed a correct letter guess. The first team to guess the expression correctly wins the game.

● La carta

Materials	◆ Stationery or notebook paper
	◆ Envelopes
Players	The entire class or a medium-size group.
Preparation	None
Procedure	Give each student a sheet of stationery (or have them use notebook paper) and an envelope. Instruct the students each to write a letter in Spanish to someone in the class but not to sign their names to the letters. Then have them each address an envelope (also in Spanish) to that person. (Try to make sure that everyone is not only writing but also receiving a letter.)
	Next, ask one or two volunteers to be the mail carriers (i.e., **el cartero** or **la cartera**) and deliver the letters. Afterward, have students read their letters aloud and try to guess who wrote them.

○ Cinco

Materials
- Blank "Cinco" pages (Master 186), one for each player
- Beans or small squares of colored paper for markers, 20 to 25 for each player

Players   The entire class or small to medium-size groups

Preparation   Copy and distribute "Cinco" pages made from Master 186 (in the *Resource and Activity Book*).

Procedure   Distribute the "Cinco" pages and tell players to write a number in each square. (The range of numbers depends on what you are teaching or practicing at a given time.) You may have players choose a square to be a "free" square by coloring it or drawing a symbol.

Call out a number, and each player with that number will put a marker on the square. When a player has covered five down, five across, or five diagonally, he or she must call out **¡Cinco!** in order to win.

Variation   Players may also write the target vocabulary words or verb forms in blank squares. If you provide a list of words from which students may choose, be sure there are more words than squares on the "Cinco" game page.

◑ Completa la categoría

Materials
- Paper and pencil for each player

Players   The entire class or medium-size to large groups.

Preparation   None

Procedure   Write a category on the chalkboard, such as one of the following:

1. **Preguntas que le haces a un agente de viajes**

2. **Mandatos que hace un maestro**

3. Cosas que dice un campeón

4. Preguntas que les hace un médico

Set a time limit. At the count of three, students write all the questions, commands, or expressions they can think of for the category. At the end of the time limit, students count the number of entries. The student with the highest number reads his or her list first. If a question, command, or expression is not appropriate or if the student has repeated an entry, it must be crossed off the list. If the student still has more than the next highest student, he or she wins. If not, the student with the next highest number reads aloud. The procedure continues until a tie is called or a winner is declared.

○ Concentración

Materials
- ◆ "Concentración" game board with pockets or bulletin board and envelopes

- ◆ Vocabulary Cards of the target vocabulary, two sets; or one set of teacher-prepared word cards and one set of the corresponding Vocabulary Cards

Players

The entire class or a medium-size group, a small group, or pairs of students.

Preparation

If the game is played with a large or medium-size group, you may wish to make a "Concentración" game board from poster board or tag board. Attach 12 to 16 pockets (four across and three or four down), making sure that each pocket allows easy access to the vocabulary or word card inside. Then number the pockets in order. (You may tack envelopes to a bulletin board for the game board, as well.)

If the game is played with a small group or in pairs, you may simply place the Vocabulary Cards face down on a table.

Either make the game cards from the target Vocabulary Card blackline masters in the *Resource and Activity Book* or make one set of Vocabulary Cards and one set of index cards on which you have printed the vocabulary words. Either way, you could include a free card **(libre)** to make the game more interesting.

Procedure

The entire class or a medium-size group. Divide the group into two teams. The first person on a team goes up to the board and pulls out a card from a pocket, saying or reading the word or phrase corresponding to that card. Then he or she pulls out another card from another pocket, saying or reading the appropriate word or phrase. If the cards match, the team gets a point, the cards are set aside, and the next team member comes up. If the cards do not match, the player returns the cards to their pockets and the other team gets a chance. When all the pockets are empty, the team with the most matched cards wins the game.

Small groups or pairs. Two sets of Vocabulary Cards or word cards may be mixed together and laid face down on a table. Students may take turns choosing cards and trying to make a match. Each time a card is turned face up, the player must say or read the appropriate word or phrase. If two cards match, the player may continue. If they do not match, the next player tries. At the end, the player with the most matched cards wins.

Conquista el mundo

Materials
- ◆ Map of North and South America
- ◆ Self-adhesive, removable notes in two colors (one color for each team)
- ◆ Teacher-prepared question cards

Players   The entire class or a medium-size group.

Preparation   On a set of index cards, write a question (in Spanish) that can be answered with a vocabulary word, verb conjugation, or preposition. The questions may range from simple to complex, depending on what you want to practice:

Uses of **Estar**

1. **Tienes sueño. No duermes bien por la noche. ¿Cómo estás?**
2. **Ven muchos animales en sus jaulas. ¿Dónde están?**

Verbs

1. **Tienes sueño. Te acuestas. ¿Qué haces? (dormirse)**
2. **Comiste el almuerzo. El camarero te da la cuenta. Luego, ¿qué pasa? (pagar)**

Object Pronouns

1. **Es tu cumpleaños. Tu amigo tiene un regalo. Tu amigo _____ da el regalo.** (indirect object pronoun)
2. **Tienes que escribir un reporte para mañana. ¿Qué vas a hacer esta noche?** (direct object pronoun)

Procedure   Divide the class or group into two teams. The first player on the starting team draws a question card. If the player responds correctly, he or she chooses a country, says its name in Spanish, and then "conquers" that country for his or her team by placing a colored self-adhesive note on the map. If the player responds incorrectly, the opposing team gets one chance to answer the same question. If their answer is correct, they may "conquer" a country; if it is incorrect, neither team gets on the map that round. The opposing team then has its chance to draw a card and "conquer" a country.

The teams continue to alternate turns until all the cards have been drawn. The team that has "conquered" the most countries at the end of the game is the winner.

○ ¿Cuánto cuesta la palabra?

Materials   ◆ "¿Cuánto cuesta la palabra?" letter sheet (Master 187), one for each student

Players   The entire class, medium-size groups, or small groups

Preparation   Make copies of Master 187 (from the *Resource and Activity Book*) and distribute them to students.

Procedure   Divide the class or group into teams. One team will say or spell a word in Spanish, and the other team will add up the values for each letter in the word and then state an amount. The letter values are printed on the letter sheet.

S1: **¿Cuánto cuesta la palabra *prima*?**

S2: **Cuesta sesenta y seis pesos.**

Point out to students that vowels with accent marks have higher values than those without. Either award a set point value for each round won or use the values of the words as the scores. Students may add up the totals at the end of the game.

Variation   To make the game more challenging, you may set letter limits for each round. Round 1 may require students to say a two-letter word; round 2, a three-letter word; and so on.

● Descripciones I

Materials
- ◆ Pictures that illustrate the target vocabulary
- ◆ Paper and pencil, one for each group

Players

Small groups or pairs of students.

Preparation

From old magazines or newspapers, compile an assortment of colorful pictures that suggest or illustrate the target vocabulary. You may wish to mount the pictures on heavy-gauge paper and laminate them for durability.

Procedure

Give a picture, a sheet of paper, and a pencil to each group. At a given signal, instruct each group to write, in Spanish, all the words or phrases they can think of to describe their picture. You may set a time limit of, perhaps, three minutes. At the end of the time limit, collect the lists of descriptions. The group that comes up with the longest list of correctly written words and phrases wins the competition.

◑ Descripciones II

Materials
- ◆ 3" x 5" index cards

Players

The entire class in small groups.

Preparation

Make, or have students make, 20 or more pairs of cards. On one card of each pair, write the name of a person (e.g., a famous athlete, actor, or president; a person well-known in the school, such as an aide). On its matching card, write four or five Spanish words or phrases that describe that person's appearance, personality, or job. Make certain that each description is distinctive and will not suit more than one person card in a set. Collect and sort the cards by pairs into sets. Then shuffle each set of cards.

Procedure   Divide the class into small groups and give each group a set of cards. Each group tries to match their name cards with the appropriate word cards. Score two points for each correct match. The winner is the group that scores the most points at the end of a time limit, such as three minutes.

○ Dibujitos

Materials
- Drawing paper and pencils

- 3" x 5" index cards

- Digital watch or clock with a second hand (or a one-minute timer)

Players   Medium-size to small groups in two teams.

Preparation   Make (or have students make) a set of game cards by writing a vocabulary word on one side of an index card. Then shuffle all the cards, and place them face down in a pile.

Procedure   Divide the group into two teams. The first player on a team takes the top card from the pile and silently reads the vocabulary word. Then, when you say **Empieza**, the player begins drawing a picture to illustrate the word on the chalkboard or a piece of drawing paper. (No letters or numbers are allowed. Players may respond to their teams with hand motions and gestures but not with words.) If the player's team guesses the word before one minute is up, the team scores one point. Then a member of the other team takes a card from the pile.

After four cards have been taken (two by each team), call a **carrera** (or race) round. During this round, one player from each team reads the vocabulary word on the next card. When you say **Empiecen**, both players begin drawing pictures to illustrate the same word. The first team to guess the word correctly wins the **carrera** round and scores five points.

At the end of the time period (eight to ten minutes), the team with the higher score wins the game.

◑ ¿Dónde estoy?

Materials
- Pictures of different locations (from old magazines or newspapers) or Vocabulary Cards of places *(Resource and Activity Book)*

- Manila folders cut in half

- Self-adhesive, removable notes (3" x 3" or larger), optional

Players
Small groups or students playing in pairs.

Preparation
Cut manila folders in half along the fold to make large, sturdy, opaque playing cards. On one side of a playing card, paste a picture of a location (e.g., a bank, an airport, a desert, a beach, etc.). On the other side, write a word, phrase, or sentence related to that place. (You may wish to write on self-adhesive removable notes instead, in order to reuse the cards later to practice other verb tenses, expressions, etc.)

Procedure
Place all the cards in a pile so that the pictures are face down. Each player, in turn, reads the word, phrase, or sentence on the top card, tries to guess where he or she would be likely to carry out the activity, and then completes the sentence: **Estoy en** (name of place). Afterward, the player turns over the card to see if he or she is correct. If correct, the player receives another turn; if not, the next player takes a turn. The player who collects the most cards wins the game.

Variation
The game may be played with larger groups in teams. A player picks up a card, without looking at it, and shows it to team members. Team members must call out items, people, or activities associated with that place. The player holding up the card has one chance to guess the location (e.g., **Estoy en el banco.**).

◐ Escoge tu número

Materials
- Vocabulary cards or teacher-prepared word cards of the target vocabulary, teacher-prepared question cards
- Game board (optional)

Players
The entire class, medium-size groups, or small groups.

Preparation
This game may be played at the chalkboard, or you may make an "Escoge tu número" game board out of poster board. Write as many categories as you wish to review across the board. Then write a column of numbers under each category to represent point values. To add interest, you may use question marks to indicate a mystery category.

La rutina	La playa	¿?
100	100	100
200	200	200
300	300	300
400	400	400
500	500	500

Select Vocabulary Cards (*Resource and Activity Book*) for the unit vocabulary you wish to review or write the vocabulary words on index cards to practice reading. If you want to make the game more challenging, write questions on the index cards (e.g., **Primero, Juan se lava la cara. Luego, Juan_____ la cara. ¿Qué hace Juan?** OR **Usas la crema de broncear. ¿Qué vas a hacer?**).

Procedure
Divide the class into two or more teams and select one player from each team to keep score. Teams alternate having a player choose a category and a point value and then identify the illustration (or read the word or answer the question) corresponding to that value. If the player responds correctly, the team receives the point value selected. If the player responds incorrectly, the other team has a chance to give the answer, as well as continue with their turn. The team that accumulates the most points wins the game.

The game may be played as time permits during a class period, or it may be extended over several class periods until a team has reached a specified number of points.

● El maratón

Materials
    ◆ None

Players
    The entire class or small groups.

Preparation
    None

Procedure
    Ask for two volunteers to be the players. Name another player as the score-keeper and have the remaining players be judges. Player A begins the game by asking a question. Player B answers the question and asks another question. Player A answers that question and asks another question. Play continues until one player cannot ask or answer a question or until one player is successfully challenged by a judge.

    As the players proceed, the scorekeeper marks one point for every **pregunta** and **respuesta** made by each player. Students at their seats may challenge a player if they think the question or the answer is incorrect. If the player is unable to correct the error by the count of ten, the challenger must correct it and then take his or her place. The player who is eliminated receives his or her score from the scorekeeper. At the end of the game, the player who has the most points is the winner.

◑ Pasapalabra

Materials
    ◆ Index cards (or slips of paper)

Players
    The entire class or a medium-size to large group.

Preparation
    Make duplicate sets of game cards by writing each of the target vocabulary words on two separate index cards.

Procedure
    Divide the class into two teams. Call two players from each team to the front of the room. Give one partner from each team a game card containing the same Spanish word. Ask one team to start the game. The player with the card

gives a one-word clue (in Spanish) to his or her partner, who then tries to guess the word on the card. If the partner guesses correctly, the team scores ten points. If not, play passes to the other team. The player with the word card gives a different one-word clue (in Spanish) to his or her partner. If the partner guesses correctly, that team scores nine points; if not, play reverts to the first team for another one-word clue, this time worth eight points. Continue play until a specified point count is reached (e.g., five or zero). Then begin a new round with another vocabulary word.

◑ ¿Quién tiene la culpa?

Materials

◆ Three large envelopes, one for each word category

◆ Vocabulary cards (blackline masters) or teacher-prepared word cards (index cards with hand-printed vocabulary words)

Players

The entire class or medium-size to large groups.

Preparation

Label each of three large envelopes with word categories such as **las personas, los lugares,** and **las cosas.** Fill each envelope with the appropriate Vocabulary Cards *(Resource and Activity Book)* or word cards.

Procedure

Select a "crime," such as breaking a window. Then call three volunteers to the front of the room. Each volunteer selects a card from a different envelope and either holds it up or walks around the room for all the students to see. The players at their seats try to solve the crime by stating who is committing it, where it takes place, and how it is done (e.g., **El piloto rompe la ventana del avión con una maleta.** OR **La camarera rompe la ventana de la agencia de viajes con unas monedas.).** The first player to piece the crime together correctly wins that round.

The game may be played as review for several rounds, or one round may be played each day for a week or so.

◐ Vamos en taxi

Materials
- Game board (Master 188)

- Number spinner (Master 189)

- Paper fastener

- Overhead projector (optional)

- Game pieces (different colored beans, plastic disks, or other markers), one for each team

- Vocabulary Cards (blackline masters) or teacher-prepared word cards (index cards with hand-printed words, phrases, or sentences)

Players

The entire class or a medium-size to large group in teams; two to four players.

Preparation

Use Master 188 *(Resource and Activity Book)* to make a transparency of the game board. Color in the blank squares and drawings. Project the transparency of the game board onto a smooth, flat surface and use different colored self-adhesive removable notes as game pieces on the projected surface (or use beans, plastic disks, etc. and place them on top of the transparency on the overhead projector).

If the game is to be played by pairs or small groups, paste a copy of Master 188 on heavy stock or cardboard and color in the blank squares and drawings. Laminate the board for durability. Use Master 189 to make a number spinner. Cut out the number circle and arrow and paste them on cardboard or heavy stock that has been cut in the same shapes. Punch a hole in the middle of the number circle and the arrow. Insert the paper fastener through the holes in the arrow and circle and then bend the ends loosely on the back.

Procedure

Divide the class into two to four teams and give each team a game piece. The object of the game is to travel by taxi through the city to reach the championship baseball game as quickly as possible. The first team to arrive wins.

The teams start at opposite ends of the game board. The players on each team take turns spinning for a number. In order to advance the specified number of spaces, the player must draw a vocabulary or word card and either identify or read it correctly. (To make the game more challenging, you may write short sentences for the players to read or make one set of noun/pronoun cards and one set of infinitive cards for students to say the verb form that corresponds to the noun or pronoun.)

Note: The game may be played as a review or closing activity of each class period for a week or more until one team wins.

El tren. One of the spaces on the number spinner is the train. When a player spins the train, the game piece is moved to the nearest train square and the team loses a turn. If a player lands on a train square on the board, the team loses a turn.

El avión, el autobús, la bicicleta. Some of the spaces on the board are marked with a plane, a bus, or a bicycle. When the player lands on these spaces, the game piece may be moved ahead two spaces if the player can correctly identify or read an additional card.

El coche de policía, la gasolinera. Some of the spaces are marked with a police car or a gas station pump. When a player lands on these spaces, he or she must go back two spaces.

● ¿Verdad o mentira?

Materials
◆ Pencil and paper for each student

Players
Small groups.

Preparation
Have each player write three statements at the top of a sheet of paper. Tell players to write two statements that are sensible and might be true and one statement that is absurd and obviously a lie. After each statement, they should write **verdad** or **mentira.**

1. **Mi papá es piloto. (mentira)**
2. **Tengo cincuenta casetes en casa. (verdad)**
3. **Tengo un salvavidas en la bañera. (mentira)**

Procedure
Each player in turn reads his or her statements aloud. The other players write the person's name and number their papers from 1 to 3. As they hear each statement, they write **lo creo** if they think it is true or **no lo creo** if they think it is false. The player with the highest number of correct guesses, after everyone has had a turn, wins the game.

Variation	To make the game more challenging, require students to write sentences based on geography, distances, etc., or require them to write sentences about past activities.

○ El volcán

Materials	◆ Game board (Master 190)
	◆ Number spinner (Master 191)
	◆ Paper fastener
	◆ Overhead projector (optional)
	◆ Game pieces (different colored beans, plastic disks, or other markers), one for each team
	◆ Vocabulary Cards (blackline masters) or teacher-prepared word cards (index cards with hand-printed words, phrases, or sentences)
Players	The entire class or a medium-size to large group in teams; two to four players.
Preparation	Use Master 190 *(Resource and Activity Book)* to make a transparency of the game board. Color in the blank squares and drawings. Project the transparency of the game board onto a smooth, flat surface and use different colored self-adhesive removable notes as game pieces on the projected surface (or use beans, plastic disks, etc. and place them on top of the transparency on the overhead projector).
	If the game is to be played by pairs or small groups, paste a copy of Master 190 on heavy stock or cardboard and color in the blank squares and drawings. Laminate the board for durability. Use Master 191 to make a number spinner. Cut out the number circle and arrow and paste them on cardboard or heavy stock that has been cut in the same shapes. Punch a hole in the middle of the number circle and the arrow. Insert the paper fastener through the holes in the arrow and circle and then bend the ends loosely on the back.

Procedure   Divide the class into two to four teams and give each team a game piece. The object of the game is to escape the erupting volcano and go through the jungle to safety on the other side of the mountains. The first team to arrive wins. The players on each team take turns spinning for a number. In order to advance the specified number of spaces, the player must draw a vocabulary or word card and either identify or read it correctly. (To make the game more challenging, you may write short sentences for the players to read or make one set of noun/pronoun cards and one set of infinitive cards for students to say the verb form that corresponds to the noun or pronoun.)

Note: The game may be played as a review or closing activity of each class period for a week or more until one team wins.

El salto de agua. One of the spaces on the number spinner is the waterfall. When a player spins the waterfall, the game piece is moved to the nearest waterfall and glides down to the adjoining space below. The only way a team can take a short-cut down the waterfall is to spin it.

La abeja. Some of the spaces on the board are marked with a bee. When a player lands on **una abeja**, the game piece may be moved ahead two spaces if the player can identify or read two cards correctly.

La serpiente. Some of the spaces on the board are marked with a snake. When a player lands on **una serpiente**, the game piece is moved back two squares.

Variation   If time is short, cover up some of the "pitfall" **(la serpiente)** squares on the board.

The ACTFL Proficiency Guidelines

In recent years, one of the key forces in foreign-language education has been the proficiency-oriented approach to the curriculum and classroom. Through grants from the U.S. Department of Education, the American Council on the Teaching of Foreign Languages (ACTFL) has developed and revised generic guidelines for assessing language proficiency in speaking, listening, reading, and writing. These guidelines describe a range of abilities: beginning at the Novice level, progressing through the Intermediate and Advanced levels, and culminating in the Superior to Distinguished levels. The descriptions are intended to be representative of the ranges of ability, not exhaustive and all-encompassing, and to apply to stages of proficiency, rather than to achievement within a specific curriculum.

In this section, you will find the descriptions of proficiency in the four skill areas that relate to the students of *¡Viva el español!*— speaking, listening, reading, and writing—at the Novice through Intermediate levels.

Generic Descriptions—Speaking

Novice
The Novice level is characterized by an ability to communicate minimally with learned material.

Novice-Low
Oral production consists of isolated words and perhaps a few high-frequency phrases. Essentially no functional communicative ability.

Novice-Mid
Oral production continues to consist of isolated words and learned phrases within very predictable areas of need, although quantity is increased. Vocabulary is sufficient only for handling simple, elementary needs and expressing basic courtesies. Utterances rarely consist of more than two or

three words and show frequent long pauses and repetition of interlocutor's words. Speaker may have some difficulty producing even the simplest utterances. Some Novice-Mid speakers will be understood only with great difficulty.

Novice-High   Able to satisfy partially the requirements of basic communicative exchanges by relying heavily on learned utterances but occasionally expanding these through simple recombinations of their elements. Can ask questions or make statements involving learned material. Shows signs of spontaneity, although this falls short of real autonomy of expression. Speech continues to consist of learned utterances rather than of personalized, situationally adapted ones. Vocabulary centers on areas such as basic objects, places, and most common kinship terms. Pronunciation may still be strongly influenced by first language. Errors are frequent and, in spite of repetition, some Novice-High speakers will have difficulty being understood even by sympathetic interlocutors.

Intermediate   The intermediate level is characterized by an ability to

— create with the language by combining and recombining learned elements, though primarily in a reactive mode;

— initiate, minimally sustain, and close in a simple way basic communicative tasks; and

— ask and answer questions.

Intermediate-Low   Able to handle successfully a limited number of interactive, task-oriented and social situations. Can ask and answer questions, initiate and respond to simple statements, and maintain face-to-face conversation, although in a highly restricted manner and with much linguistic inaccuracy. Within these limitations can perform such tasks as introducing self, ordering a meal, asking directions, and making purchases. Vocabulary is adequate to express only the most elementary needs. Strong interference from native language may occur. Misunderstandings frequently arise, but with repetition, the Intermediate-Low speaker can generally be understood by sympathetic interlocutors.

Intermediate-Mid	Able to handle successfully a variety of uncomplicated, basic and communicative tasks and social situations. Can talk simply about self and family members. Can ask and answer questions and participate in simple conversations on topics beyond the most immediate needs: e.g., personal history and leisure-time activities. Utterance length increases slightly, but speech may continue to be characterized by frequent long pauses, since the smooth incorporation of even basic conversational strategies is often hindered as the speaker struggles to create appropriate language forms. Pronunciation may continue to be strongly influenced by first language and fluency may still be strained. Although misunderstandings still arise, the Intermediate-Mid speaker can generally be understood by sympathetic interlocutors.
Intermediate-High	Able to handle successfully most uncomplicated communicative tasks and social situations. Can initiate, sustain, and close a general conversation with a number of strategies appropriate to a range of circumstances and topics, but errors are evident. Limited vocabulary still necessitates hesitation and may bring about slightly unexpected circumlocution. There is emerging evidence of connected discourse, particularly for simple narrative and/or description. The Intermediate-High speaker can generally be understood even by interlocutors not accustomed to dealing with speaking at this level, but repetition may still be required.

Generic Descriptions—Listening

	These guidelines assume that all listening tasks take place in an authentic environment at a normal rate of speech using standard or near-standard norms.
Novice-Low	Understanding is limited to occasional isolated words, such as cognates, borrowed words, and high-frequency social conventions. Essentially no ability to comprehend even short utterances.

Novice-Mid
Able to understand some short, learned utterances, particularly where context strongly supports understanding and speech is clearly audible. Comprehends some words and phrases from simple questions, statements, high-frequency commands, and courtesy formulae about topics that refer to basic personal information or the immediate physical setting. The listener requires long pauses for assimilation and periodically requests repetition and/or a slower rate of speech.

Novice-High
Able to understand short, learned utterances and some sentence-length utterances, particularly where context strongly supports understanding and speech is clearly audible. Comprehends words and phrases from simple questions, statements, high-frequency commands, and courtesy formulae. May require repetition, rephrasing, and/or a slowed rate of speech for comprehension.

Intermediate-Low
Able to understand sentence-length utterances which consist of recombinations of learned elements in a limited number of content areas, particularly if strongly supported by the situational context. Content refers to basic personal background and needs, social conventions, and routine tasks, such as getting meals and receiving simple instructions and directions. Listening tasks pertain primarily to spontaneous face-to-face conversations. Understanding is often uneven; repetition and rewording may be necessary. Misunderstandings in both main ideas and details arise frequently.

Intermediate-Mid
Able to understand sentence-length utterances which consist of recombinations of learned utterances on a variety of topics. Content continues to refer primarily to basic personal background and needs, social conventions, and somewhat more complex tasks, such as lodging, transportation, and shopping. Additional content areas include some personal interests and activities, and a greater diversity of instructions and directions. Listening tasks not only pertain to spontaneous face-to-face conversations but also to short routine telephone conversations and some deliberate speech, such as simple announcements and reports over the media. Understanding continues to be uneven.

Intermediate-High
Able to sustain understanding over longer stretches of connected discourse on a number of topics pertaining to different times and places; however, understanding is inconsistent due to failure to grasp main ideas and/or details. Thus, while topics do not differ significantly from those of an Advanced-level listener, comprehension is less in quantity and poorer in quality.

Generic Descriptions—Reading

These guidelines assume all reading texts to be authentic and legible.

Novice-Low
Able occasionally to identify isolated words and/or major phrases when strongly supported by context.

Novice-Mid
Able to recognize the symbols of an alphabetic and/or syllabic writing system and/or a limited number of characters in a system that uses characters. The reader can identify an increasing number of highly contextualized words and/or phrases including cognates and borrowed words, where appropriate. Material understood rarely exceeds a single phrase at a time, and rereading may be required.

Novice-High
Has sufficient control of the writing system to interpret written language in areas of practical need. Where vocabulary has been learned, can read for instructional and directional purposes standardized messages, phrases, or expressions, such as some items on menus, schedules, timetables, maps, and signs. At times, but not on a consistent basis, the Novice-High-level reader may be able to derive meaning from material at a slightly higher level where context and/or extralinguistic background knowledge are supportive.

Intermediate-Low	Able to understand main ideas and/or some facts from the simplest connected texts dealing with basic personal and social needs. Such texts are linguistically noncomplex and have a clear underlying internal structure, for example, chronological sequencing. They impart basic information about which the reader has to make only minimal suppositions or to which the reader brings personal interest and/or knowledge. Examples include messages with social purposes or information for the widest possible audience, such as public announcements and short, straightforward instructions dealing with public life. Some misunderstandings will occur.
Intermediate-Mid	Able to read consistently with increased understanding simple connected texts dealing with a variety of basic and social needs. Such texts are still linguistically noncomplex and have a clear underlying internal structure. They impart basic information about which the reader has to make minimal suppositions and to which the reader brings personal interest and/or knowledge. Examples may include short, straightforward descriptions of persons, places, and things written for a wide audience.
Intermediate-High	Able to read consistently with full understanding simple connected texts dealing with basic personal and social needs about which the reader has personal interest and/or knowledge. Can get some main ideas and information from texts at the next higher level featuring description and narration. Structural complexity may interfere with comprehension; for example, basic grammatical relations may be misinterpreted and temporal references may rely primarily on lexical items. Has some difficulty with the cohesive factors in discourse, such as matching pronouns with referents. While texts do not differ significantly from those at the Advanced level, comprehension is less consistent. May have to read material several times for understanding.

Generic Descriptions—Writing

Novice-Low	Able to form some letters in an alphabetic system. In languages whose writing systems use syllabaries or characters, writer is able to both copy and produce the basic strokes. Can produce romanization of isolated characters, where applicable.

Novice-Mid   Able to copy or transcribe familiar words or phrases and reproduce some from memory. No practical communicative writing skills.

Novice-High   Able to write simple fixed expressions and limited memorized material and some recombinations thereof. Can supply information on simple forms and documents. Can write names, numbers, dates, own nationality, and other simple autobiographical information, as well as some short phrases and simple lists. Can write all the symbols in an alphabetic or syllabic system or 50–100 characters or compounds in a character writing system. Spelling and representation of symbols (letters, syllables, characters) may be partially correct.

Intermediate-Low   Able to meet limited practical writing needs. Can write short messages, postcards, and take down simple notes, such as telephone messages. Can create statements or questions within the scope of limited language experience. Material produced consists of recombinations of learned vocabulary and structures into simple sentences on very familiar topics. Language is inadequate to express in writing anything but elementary needs. Frequent errors in grammar, vocabulary, punctuation, spelling, and in formation of nonalphabetic symbols, but writing can be understood by natives used to the writing of nonnatives.

Intermediate-Mid   Able to meet a number of practical writing needs. Can write short, simple letters. Content involves personal preferences, daily routine, everyday events, and other topics grounded in personal experience. Can express present time or at least one other time frame or aspect consistently, e.g., nonpast, habitual, imperfective. Evidence of control of the syntax of noncomplex sentences and basic inflectional morphology, such as declensions and conjugation. Writing tends to be a loose collection of sentences or sentence fragments on a given topic and provides little evidence of conscious organization. Can be understood by natives used to the writing of nonnatives.

Intermediate-High

Able to meet most practical writing needs and limited social demands. Can take notes in some detail on familiar topics and respond in writing to personal questions. Can write simple letters, brief synopses and paraphrases, summaries of biographical data, work and school experience. In those languages relying primarily on content words and time expressions to express time, tense, or aspect, some precision is displayed; where tense and/or aspect is expressed through verbal inflection, forms are produced rather consistently, but not always accurately. An ability to describe and narrate in paragraphs is emerging. Rarely uses basic cohesive elements, such as pronominal substitutions or synonyms in written discourse. Writing, though faulty, is generally comprehensible to natives used to the writing of nonnatives.

SCOPE AND SEQUENCE

UNIDAD DE REPASO

Communication

Review of expressions and vocabulary
learned in *¿Qué tal?*, including talking
about

what the parts of the body are

what someone is wearing

how someone's clothes look

what a person is like

what someone is doing

what is inside a house or apartment

what someone's house looks like

what is in a kitchen

what fruits someone likes

what someone wants to eat for breakfast,
lunch, or dinner

what time someone eats breakfast, lunch, or dinner

what activities someone can do

Structures	Culture
Review of structures learned in *¿Qué tal?*, including • use of **doler** • agreement of gender and number • interrogatives • comparative **más/menos...que** • use of **estar** for location • use of **gustar** • uses of **querer** + infinitive, **tener que** + infinitive, **poder** + infinitive, and **pensar** + infinitive • telling time • reflexive verbs • superlatives	Learn about the custom of embracing friends in Spanish-speaking cultures Learn examples of the close ties between the United States and the Spanish-speaking world

UNIDAD 1

Communication

Talking about playing sports

¿Quieres jugar al tenis?
No, no puedo. Voy a jugar al fútbol con los
muchachos.

el baloncesto	el equipo
el béisbol	la jugadora
el fútbol	el jugador
el fútbol americano	
el tenis	
el volibol	

Talking about pastimes

¿Qué te gusta hacer los fines de semana?
Bueno, mi pasatiempo favorito es montar
a caballo.

el ajedrez
las damas
el dominó
los juegos electrónicos

ir de pesca
ir en bicicleta
montar a caballo
sacar fotos
tocar un instrumento
cultivar plantas
coleccionar estampillas

Structures	Culture
Conjugation of **u** to **ue** stem-changing verb **jugar** in present tense	Learn about the popularity of soccer in the Spanish-speaking world
Use of **a** after **jugar**; distinction between **jugar** and **tocar**	Learn that parks in Spain and Latin America often have areas set aside for the public to play board games
Use of **¿cuál?** (recycled)	Learn about tennis and tennis stars in Spanish-speaking countries
Adjectives describing personality (recycled)	
Review conjugation of **ser**; introduce **nosotros** form of **ser**	

UNIDAD 2

Talking about professions and
what people do on their jobs

¿Qué hace tu tía Amalia?
Ella es médica. Examina a los pacientes.

¿Quién trabaja en la estación de bomberos?
Los bomberos. Ellos apagan los incendios.

¿Qué quieres ser?
Quiero ser dueña de una compañía.

¿Qué hace tu mamá?
Es una policía. Ayuda a la gente.

el hospital	el almacén
el médico	el vendedor
la médica	la vendedora
la paciente	
el paciente	

la estación de bomberos
el bombero
la bombera

el departamento de policía
la policía
el policía
la gente

la compañía	el empleado
el dueño	la fábrica
la dueña	la obrera
la empleada	el obrero

Talking about knowing
people

¿Conoces a la Sra. Velasco?
Sí, conozco a la Sra. Velasco.

Structures	Culture
Conjugation and use of **conocer**; use of personal **a** with **conocer**	Find out about Spanish-speaking communities in the United States
Present tense of **–ar**, **–er**, and **–ir** verbs (recycled)	Learn about pre-Columbian plazas in Latin America
Use of present progressive; formation of present participle for **–ar**, **–er**, and **–ir** verbs	Learn about a place in many smaller towns where people gather to discuss local events
	Use **el bombero** as an example of how languages can describe the same job in different ways
	Learn about the value of bilingual employees to businesses in the United States

UNIDAD 3

Communication

Talking about getting around
in the city

¿Dónde está la parada de autobús?
Está en la avenida, cerca del semáforo.

¿Cómo vamos a la farmacia?
Vamos en autobús.

abrochar los cinturones
la avenida
el autobús
la calle
el coche
la chofera
la farmacia
la gasolinera
la parada de autobús
los semáforos
el taxista
el taxi

el centro
el rascacielos   **los edificios**
la plaza   **el teatro**
ir a pie   **el estacionamiento**
los automóviles **el mercado**

Giving directions

Dobla a la izquierda en la avenida Cisneros.

a la izquierda
derecho
a la derecha

Structures	Culture
Command forms for **tú** of **–ar**, **–er**, and **–ir** verbs; uses of command forms	Find out that some of the world's largest cities are in Latin America
Conjugations of **e** to **i** stem-changing verbs **pedir**, **servir**, and **seguir**; uses of **pedir**	Through the example of architecture in Spanish cities, learn about the Arabic cultural heritage in the Spanish-speaking world
	Learn that people living in cities in Spanish-speaking countries often make use of efficient subway systems

UNIDAD 4

Communication

Talking about traveling	**¿A qué hora sale el tren?** **A las siete. Tengo que estar en la estación** **de ferrocarriles a las cinco y media.**
	Vamos a México en avión. **Voy al centro en tren.** **Van a Puerto Rico en barco.**

el avión **el barco** **el aeropuerto**
el puerto **el tren**
la estación de ferrocarriles

Talking about countries

¿Cuáles son los países de la América del Norte?
¿Dónde está Colombia?
Está en la América del Sur.
¿Hablan español en Puerto Rico?

la América del Norte	la América del Sur	
el Canadá	la Argentina	Bolivia
los Estados Unidos	Chile	Colombia
México	el Ecuador	el Paraguay
	el Perú	el Uruguay
	Venezuela	

la América Central y el Caribe		
Belice	Costa Rica	Cuba
Guatemala	Haití	Honduras
Nicaragua	el Panamá	Puerto Rico
El Salvador	la República Dominicana	

Europa	España

Asking and telling
nationalities

Pepe y Yolanda son ecuatorianos. ¿De dónde son?
Ellos son del Ecuador.

Structures

Names of nationalities written in lower-case letters; agreement of gender and number; **ser** used with nationalities; definite article needed with certain countries

Recycle agreement of gender and number; recycle conjugation of **ser**; recycle use of **estar** for location

Uses of preposition **en**

Use of **de** to indicate where someone is from

Culture

Learn how some people in Spanish-speaking countries make their living selling food and beverages to train and bus passengers

Find out about Spain's railroad system, and about train travel in Latin America

Learn about the Panama Canal and why it is important

Learn one way that a map's perspective is relative rather than absolute

UNIDAD 5

Communication

Talking about taking a trip

¿Adónde quieren ir ustedes?
Queremos viajar al volcán.

la agencia de viajes
el viajero
la viajera
el agente de viajes
la agente de viajes
descansar

Discussing travel destinations

el desierto
el lago
las montañas
la playa
el río
la selva
el valle
el volcán

Arranging a trip and discussing
how much it costs

Señorita, ¿cuesta mucho un viaje a la playa?
No, no cuesta mucho. Cuesta seiscientos dólares.

Quiero pasar las vacaciones en la playa.
El viaje va a costar ochocientos dólares.

el billete
costar
pagar

Structures	Culture
Review conjugations of regular **–ar**, **–er**, and **–ir** verbs, such as **visitar**, **correr** and **recibir**	Learn that Latin America has diverse ecosystems and terrains
Conjugations of **estar**, **ser**, and **ir**	Learn that Castilian Spanish is only one of four languages spoken in Spain
Conjugations of an **o** to **ue** stem-changing verb **(poder)**, and an **e** to **ie** stem-changing verb **(pensar)**	Find out about some dramatic geographical features of Latin America—including the highest mountains in the Americas and one of the driest deserts in the world
Numbers (recycled)	
Telling the time when an event or activity occurs (recycled)	

UNIDAD 6

Communication

Traveling by airplane	**Tenemos que hacer fila con los otros pasajeros.** **Aquí está mi maleta.**
	¿Qué está haciendo la aeromoza? **Está hablando con un pasajero.**
	El asiento es cómodo.

el aeromozo	**la aeromoza**
cómodo	**incómodo**
el equipaje	
el pasajero	**la pasajera**
el piloto	**la piloto**
hacer fila	
la maleta	
la línea aérea	
los asientos	

Talking about traveling in terms of schedules, arrivals, and departures	
despegar	**aterrizar**
volar	
el horario	
llegadas	**salidas**
el vuelo	
la puerta	
a tiempo	
tarde	**temprano**

Structures	Culture
Conjugation of **hacer** in present tense	Learn about how Latin Americans must rely on air travel because of the ruggedness or expanse of the terrain
Uses of **decir** and **decir que**; conjugation of **decir** in present tense	Learn that many people working in international airlines and airports in Spanish-speaking countries may speak English in addition to Spanish
Numbers and times (recycled)	
Direct object pronouns **lo**, **la**, **los**, **las**, **me**, **nos**, and **te**	Learn that La Paz, Bolivia, is built at an unusually high altitude
Use of the verb **ver** in the third person plural	Learn about the twenty-four-hour clock used for travel schedules in Spanish-speaking countries
	Learn some funny and sometimes frustrating tongue twisters in Spanish

UNIDAD 7

Communication

Arriving at a hotel

¿Necesitan un cuarto, señor?
Sí, queremos una habitación grande lejos
del ascensor.

el turista
la turista
el ascensor
las habitaciones
la llave
las tarjetas postales

Talking about things you find
in hotel rooms and elsewhere

¿Qué necesita usted?
Necesito una toalla, por favor.
La ducha todavía no tiene agua caliente.

el arte...	la cama...
antiguo	blanda
moderno	dura

la sábana
la manta

las toallas	el agua...
el jabón	caliente
la bañera	fría
la ducha	

Structures	Culture
Reflexive verbs such as **bañarse**, **ponerse**, and **dormirse**; other reflexive verbs (recycled)	Learn about the rating system often used for hotels in the Spanish-speaking world
Adjective agreement (recycled)	Find out about hotels in Spain that were once castles
Review of stem-changing verbs **jugar**, **querer**, **almorzar**, and **pedir**	Learn that guests in some hotels must share a bathroom with other guests
	Learn why motels are less common than hotels in Latin America
	Learn about **pensiones** or **fondas**
	Learn an old folk song popular throughout the Spanish-speaking world

UNIDAD 8

Communication

Changing money at a bank

Necesito dinero. Primero, voy al banco.
Vamos, hay una ventanilla abierta a la izquierda.

¿Qué vas a pedir a la cajera?
Billetes de cien pesos y algunas monedas...

Yo prefiero ahorrar mi dinero.

el banco	**la ventanilla**	**cambiar**
los billetes	**abierta**	**gastar**
el cajero	**cerrada**	**ahorrar**
la cajera		
las monedas		

Dining in a restaurant

¿Te gusta el restaurante?
El menú es interesante...

¿Vas a pedir la cuenta?
Sí, y voy a darle a la camarera una buena propina.

el restaurante
la cuenta
el camarero
la camarera
el menú
la propina

Structures	Culture
Indirect object pronouns **le**, **les**, **nos**, **me**, and **te**	Learn about **casas de cambio**
Conjugation of **dar**; uses of **dar**	Learn how tipping in restaurants is often handled in Spanish-speaking countries
	Learn that many restaurants in the Spanish-speaking world have tables outdoors where people enjoy dining
	Learn about various kinds of currency used in Latin America
	Learn about the custom in restaurants of ordering from **el menú del día**
	Learn some useful expressions with the verb **dar**

UNIDAD 9

Arranging to meet someone in the city	**Te veo en la plaza a las cuatro.**
	Me puedes buscar cerca de la fuente, delante de la alcaldía.
	¿Dónde te busco el lunes?
	Me puedes buscar cerca de la escultura.
	la alcaldía
	la escultura
	la fuente
	la iglesia
	el monumento
	el museo
	la plaza

Talking about places in the city	**¿Dónde viven muchas personas?**
	Viven en un edificio de apartamentos.
	el colegio
	el edificio de apartamentos
	el estadio
	el mercado al aire libre
	el metro
	la sinagoga
	el supermercado
	el zoológico

Talking about how people feel	**¿Cómo está Patricia?**		
	Está cansada, pero contenta.		
	contento	**cansado**	**enojado**
	triste	**confundido**	**nervioso**

Structures	Culture
Direct and indirect object pronouns with infinitives	Learn about the importance of public transportation in cities of the Spanish-speaking world
Review uses of **estar**, including in statements about how people are feeling	Find out about **el Zócalo** in Mexico City
Present progressive of **-ar**, **-er**, and **-ir** verbs (recycled)	Learn that names of many places in Latin America come from indigenous languages
Use of adverbial phrases such as **a la derecha** in giving directions	Learn about the conquest of Spain by the Arabs and about some of the architectural achievements of the Arabs in Spain
	Learn about open-air markets in the Spanish-speaking world
	Learn about a prominent figure in the Latin American independence movement

UNIDAD 10

Describing places and their location	**¿Dónde está tu casa?** **Está cerca de la esquina.** **el paso de peatones** **la esquina** **la manzana** **una cuadra** **el farol** **el norte** **el sur** **el este** **el oeste**
Getting and giving directions and finding your way around	**Perdón, señora. ¿Queda adelante o atrás el almacén?** **Gracias, señora. Tengo que encontrarme con mi papá.** **¿Cómo es el tráfico aquí?** **Por las mañanas va despacio.** **Queda...** **adelante** **atrás** **Va...** **rápido** **perderse** **despacio** **encontrarse**
Talking about measurements and distances	**metros** **kilómetros** **millas**

Structures	Culture
Familiar command forms of **–ar**, **–er**, and **–ir** verbs, such as **mirar**, **correr** and **abrir**	Learn that the metric system is used in Spanish-speaking countries for talking about distances
Familiar command forms of reflexive verbs	Find out where to buy a city map in a Spanish-speaking city
Negative familiar command forms	Learn how to get directions in Mexico City's **Zona Rosa**
Use of **quedar** to indicate location	Learn why streets in the oldest parts of many cities in Spain are barely wide enough for a single car
Interrogatives: **¿a cuántos/as?**	Find out that in some Latin American cities, the same street can have different names
	Learn some Spanish sayings

UNIDAD 11

Communication

Going shopping and
buying gifts

Tengo que comprar un regalo para mi mamá.
¿A ella le gustan los collares?
¿Algo en especial, señor?
Sí. Quiero ver los collares.

la joyería
el joyero
la joyera
las joyas
el regalo
el brazalete
el collar
el llavero

¿Son baratos o caros los zapatos?
El zapatero dice que cuestan setenta
y cinco dólares.

la zapatería	**la tienda de discos**
el zapatero	**el disco**
las bolsas	**el disco compacto**
el cinturón	**el casete**
los zapatos	
las sandalias	
barato	**caro**

Structures	Culture
Past tense of regular -ar verbs; past tense of **comprar**	Learn about some examples of high-quality goods produced in Spanish-speaking countries
Past tense of irregular –ar verbs **pagar**, **llegar**, **sacar**, **pensar**, **almorzar**, and **jugar**	Find out that young people in Latin America also enjoy going to shopping malls
Use of adverbial phrases such as **ayer** and **el año pasado** with the past tense	Learn that jewelry crafted in Latin America is often based on designs from indigenous cultures
	Learn about the multiple roles played by **zapaterías** in many Spanish-speaking countries

UNIDAD 12

Communication

Talking about going to the beach
and things you find there

¿Qué cosas traes a la playa?
Bueno, traigo una sombrilla.

¿Vas a traer la crema de broncear a la playa?
¡Claro que sí!

bronceado	**bronceada**
quemado	**quemada**
los anteojos	
la crema de broncear	
el salvavidas	
la sombrilla	
tomar el sol	

la arena
los caracoles
las conchas
el mar
¡Peligro!
¡Se prohibe nadar!

Discussing activities
you do in the water

¿Qué te gusta hacer en el mar?
Me gusta bucear.

el barco de vela
el esquí acuático
la lancha
las olas
flotar
bucear

Structures	Culture
Past tense of regular **–er** and **–ir** verbs, using **correr** and **salir** as models	Learn that Spain's beaches attract people from around the world
Use of the past tense with **o** to **ue** stem-changing verbs such as **volver**	Find out about cliff divers on the Pacific coast of Mexico
Demonstrative adjectives **este**, **ese**, **aquel**, **estos**, **esos**, **aquellos**	Learn what sports young people in Spanish-speaking enjoy playing on the beaches in their countries
Uses of **para**	Find out about surfing in Costa Rica
Gustar + infinitive and **querer** + infinitive (recycled)	Learn about a few unique seafood dishes enjoyed in Spanish-speaking countries
	Read a passage about the discovery of a Spanish ship full of treasure that sank in 1622

Teacher's Notes